G000070507

BEYOND LLAMAS, RAINBOWS & YEAR-END PARTIES

Effective and collaborative **HR**
throughout the employee journey

Beyond llamas, rainbows & year-end parties

This book wouldn't have seen the light of day without the support and love of four key people: Ricardo "Cheerio" Zuazo, who believes in me beyond measure and is my personal 24/7 cheerleader; Fe Martinez, who had the patience and drive to edit these pages; Megumi Watanabe, who brought her talent to transform my ideas and bad drawings into illustrations; and Isabel Loaldi for her encouragement through time and distance.

To all those who took a bet on getting this book, I hope it sparks in you the interest on returning the focus where it belongs: in trusting people, collaborating and willing to give things a go without fear.

LUCiA ABUGATTAS B.

CONTENTS

iNTRODUCTiON

Around eleven years ago, I stumbled upon an article that scarred me for life. Keith H. Hammonds' "Why We Hate HR" said a lot of painful things about HR practitioners. Things like those who work in HR aren't the sharpest tools in the box, that there's a reason why the best and brightest don't go into HR, that they might get a seat at the business table but are neither strategists nor leaders, that they don't really know how they add value and let alone what they are supposed to deliver for the business. Those and other statements bruised my frail HR star wannabe—with only booksmarts—ego.

If he was right, this would mean that HR is no good for anything else other than a soft and fluffy approach (just like llamas!), painting rainbows on the walls with the organization's values, and organizing year-end parties and throwing confetti. I felt that wasn't me, because I did think I was smart enough, I was even the brightest tack within my university box when it came to grades. I started to feel that I didn't want to specialize in organizational psychology anymore, because, and let's be honest, chances were I would end up in HR. If not being good enough or being average was the perception attached to the role, I didn't want it. Should I have stayed in journalism which was my first career choice? Should I switch to business management? Or maybe Finance? Spoiler alert if you've read my professional blurb: I didn't switch, which brings me to how I got here...

Through my first internship in consulting and my first real paying job as a Human Resources analyst, I started using not only my book smarts from university but also started packing up some street smarts. And while I was doing that, I bumped into more and more Mr. Hammonds. They were mostly senior employees who had a lot to complain about HR. They would ask "Why is it taking you so long to recruit one person for an IT role?" (YOU try getting that unicorn of a person in two weeks, Janet. And with that salary!). Or, "You guys don't get anything, not the people and definitely not the business" (Care to elaborate and share how it is, John?). "Why should I care about the results of the engagement survey?" (Because yes, Patricia). And my personal favorite: "It's pretty quick, just send some comms and roll a training this week". (Thanks Oscar! - You've been watching too much Oprah: You get a training, she gets a training, everybody gets a training).

As much as I didn't like what I read or heard about HR–and felt personally scarred and victimized by it, just like all those victimized by Regina George on "Mean Girls" (If you haven't seen the movie, do yourself a favor and watch it. You will be amazed of how similar some workplaces are to a high school)–, in the grand scheme of things, all these scars ended up having a strangely positive impact in my professional life. Without knowing at first, I had made it my mission (and still is) to change this perception of HR and people within the "softer" side of business, and this is something that has also tainted my change management role in consulting.

Part of this mission has been to work in a way that my deliverables and projects are well organized, with clear plans and indicators for success. This last point for example has been key by turning qualitative feedback into quantitative data that can catch the eye of a Finance or Tech person. All this to make sure that I would add value for my clients and internal stakeholders, which is only achieved by understanding their expectations and gauging their perception of the work I was doing, and taking onboard ideas that would make it better. Yes, indicators, data and feedback are key, but I've also kept in mind that there's absolutely nothing wrong with throwing in some color and pretty pictures on your PowerPoints and Excel spreadsheets (hurts no one and gets the audiences' attention!). Of course, this doesn't mean that everyone I've worked with now loves HR or is an advocate for the value of Change Management, but I like to think that at least one of the initiatives we worked on made sense to them, showed them how important this work actually is, and why they should invest on it.

Over the past years I've come to agree with Mr. Hammonds and the other Hammonds wannabes, more than what my twenty-year-old self would believe. I've even referenced him several times at work: HR and business strategy should be joined at the hip.

Let's face it, most human resources professionals are very much not interested in, nor are good at, understanding the business. We've earned that bad reputation when we've launched a training that wasn't fit for the audience and had awful feedback; when we filled a vacancy with someone who left the business within a month; or when we didn't deliver real and sustainable change for a transformation program.

I wouldn't say I'm *amazing* at understanding the businesses or industries I've worked in, but I would say I've gotten *better* at it. My journey has been interesting alright, but it has also been hard. Tech, business management, project management and finance topics are not my strong suits, but I've had to wear them. They were definitely itchy and uncomfortable suits, and God knows I've had to stretch the fabric of my poor brain to get outside my comfort zone. And while I was doing the stretching, I couldn't help feeling scared of the uncertainty, the constant feeling that I was being tested and ultimately, that I was not good enough for it.

People who know me personally and people that I have worked with know that I am not 100% tech nor finance nor business administration savvy. But they also know that I'm willing to learn and give things a go (remember: #FailFastFailOften). I might cry sometimes and complain about it in the process, but that's just a personal trait and a normal coping mechanism! (am I right?).

When it comes to core HR, I've managed to build an internal communications area from scratch (including indicators to go along!) and to design onboarding processes that have endured the test of time. From a Change Management perspective, I've accomplished to understand, support and manage people changes coming along system implementations with good results; I've also given process design a try by leveraging the famous as-is, identifying pain points and supporting the to-be process proposal. I'm also not Tech savvy, but got myself a "SAP for Dummies" and read the sh*t out of it with no shame while working on my first SAP Implementation (Plus, made good friends with some brilliant people at all levels within the organization that helped me be a part of the conversation, and even had a seat at the grown-ups table alongside the Hammonds!).

Another thing that I've come to understand is that sometimes it's healthy to pick the battles that matter when it comes to showing the value of the HR or Change Management functions. Despite all the research and the 1,310,000,000 results that Google throws when searching "Why HR is important" or the 3,100,000,000 results on "Why is Change Management important" people might *not* be interested at all. And that is OK (take a deep breath with me)

Being OK with this is not equal to not caring. It means letting go of your passion and *need* for converting everyone into HR/Change Management lovers. For me, this became quite real when I had to gather the courage to walk out of a high paying job because my work was not valued as anything more than a "nice to have", and it didn't matter how much I worked on quality deliverables, how organized, helpful and professional people thought I was.

There was never time for any people initiatives (but that's a #DramaLlama for another time).

Some people suggested I should wait a couple of years before publishing anything "Get some more professional stripes", they said. This is absolutely valid because I still have a lot to learn in my professional journey but at the same time...why wait? Can't we all share what we've learned at any stage of our lives? Isn't it better to make something rather than nothing at all because we want it to be perfect? (Also, guess how many books do you think those naysayers have published? Zero! Nada!). Meanwhile, all the way across the Atlantic in Buenos Aires, my mentor was wearing a full-on cheerleader uniform; alongside my husband right next to me in London (who would happen to look great in a cheerleading uniform). That support system was more than enough to shut the Zero Nadas. Plus, I'm learning well from Sarah Knight on how to spend my f*ck budget (meaning: where I decide to put my time, energy and money)

Making something and getting it out even if it's flawed is taking a big risk, but it's also the way of to get good results and apply my personal motto of "sharing is caring". This is exactly why I'm a big fan of Design Thinking (a framework that helps us solve problems through collaboration, engagement and creativity) and Agile Methodologies (deliver quickly!). Renzo and Isabel (who were my mentors for Design Thinking and Change Management), taught me well about the importance of both, especially on observing, reflecting and making things happen. So... WELCOME TO ITERATION 1 OF "BEYOND LLAMAS, RAINBOWS AND YEAR-END PARTIES", and bear with me because it's faaaaar from perfect.

There's a high demand for Agile methodologies and Design Thinking frameworks. And I like to think that in a way, they have brought back the "softness" and the empathic approach to the spotlight by giving it the value it deserves. This makes the person the core of the initiatives, and requires a willingness to understand why we do what we do and how we should do it. It also brings collaboration (another "softy" skill) to the table, alongside other aspects that we will likely label as "hard skills" (data analysis, coding, testing, planning, measuring).

My eyes twinkle when I hear people throwing the words "persona", "empathy map", "journey map", and even "scrum" (despite not being used correctly– you know who you are, RB!). This means that either they're starting to listen and care, or that at least they don't want to be left out of the Design Thinking/ Agile business trend. Even if it's option B, I'm happy because it's inevitable that something will resonate and inspire them to do things better. Even Wilmer from IT has a heart (and some very strong feelings when people ask him why the Internet is not working and when it will come back).

In this book you will find a mix of book and street smarts on HR, the basics of User Experience (UX), a dive into Employee Experience (EX) and its journey from pre-onboarding to the exit. I promise this whole HR / UX / EX gibberish will make sense soon enough.

I also need to address the big Cs that are embedded across the employee journey and impact the organization as a whole: Culture and Change. You will have to deal with different organizational cultures throughout your employment life, and you better know that the only constant thing within any organization will always be change. Once we're done with these two Cs (Which I like to call "The heart of it all"), we will get into a mindset of "Ready, set, go!" to take action and create an effective and collaborative experience for the employees (or peers, or line managers, whatever your audience is!).

There's no better way to start this journey for me than to get in touch with what I think and feel (see how I'm walking the talk here?). I think this book will be helpful and simple, and hope it will be more fun than a traditional Human Resources or Change Management book. I feel excited, scared, but especially thankful. Thankful to the people that have made this book possible with their generosity, support, constructive -and sometimes destructive- criticism at different stages of my professional life.

So thank you Natalie Agois, Laura Blake, Ernesto Cok, Lucia Escalante, Karen Fox, Liliana Galvan, Giannina Gutierrez, MC Gonzales, Roxana Miranda, Renzo Molina, Isabel Loaldi and Monica Velarde. You've managed to shape my professional journey in many ways. You will forever have my fluffy and rainbow side first and foremost, and if we work together again, you will also get my hard work, zero chill, excel-organized Lucia. I also need to mention and thank Lizzie Henson and Paul Fielder, who created the HR Ninjas in the UK, an effective and collaborative Facebook group for HR professionals to share their experience (We're more than 6,000 now!). Their motto "Stronger Together" is a real thing, and a fantastic one! (Which is very aligned to my personal favorite "Sharing is caring")

And last, but not least, thank you Amazon! Anyone can become a writer now. Even if you're like me and are scared sh*tless while doing it, use it as fuel despite the likely scenario that the book will only be bought by my parents and siblings (both biological and chosen ones) to keep next to your printed thesis.

Mely and Pepe, you can now say: "Our daughter wrote a whole book". So here goes nothing!

UXING THE SH*T OUT OF EX

While I was watching the second season of Friends and trying to learn the words to "This is how we do it" by Montell Jordan, Donald Norman was busy with more important things like coining the concept "User Experience" (UX).

For Norman, the first requirement for what he calls an "exemplary user experience" is to meet the exact needs of the customer without fuss, by making the products (or services) simple and elegant so that they produce joy, and even delight. You also need a multidisciplinary approach to make sure you're covering all the customer's needs.

A fun fact I discovered (thanks to Career Foundry's website) is that UX can be traced back to ancient China and ancient Greece (I sh*t you not). 6,000 years ago the Feng Shui (which translates to wind and water), was already on it by identifying and exploring how the spatial arrangement of objects related to the flow of energy among people. And around the 5th Century BC, Greek civilizations designed their workplaces and stools based on ergonomics (the way we interact with objects mankind has made).

Both cases were up to something that was not named UX just yet, but they were carefully studying how people experience certain things and how they feel about them, and ultimately, discovering what works best for them.

Kate Rand summarized in her article "Revolutionizing the Employee experience" how UX can be successfully used for EX. She starts by mentioning

HR's bad reputation (of course! Joining Hammonds' club), and how it's up to the people specialists to understand that employee engagement is vital to create an effective organization. The key for this is plugging back in the most important resources: people. This can be achieved through User Experience tools and techniques, such as Experience or Journey mapping, collaborative design, design thinking, user research, design sprints/agile approach.

McKinsey has been very straightforward on the importance of Employee Experience now and in the future. In a prophetic way, they said: "Mark our words: Employee Experience is the new standard for defining how companies should interact with their people." They are 100% right. This movement towards a more human-centered interaction makes the employees a key element in designing what works best for them (and for the organization, of course!), leading to collaborative solutions and driving organizational performance. If we nail EX, individuals will do purposeful work for meaningful recognition, managers will provide regular feedback to their teams and the teams will be empowered to make decisions.

Think about it this way: if you're asked for your opinion on something (and let's admit it, we LOVE giving our opinion), and when we share it people start building up on that idea and thinking about the impact it can have, wouldn't you be interested in making it happen? Later on, you can proudly say that it was your baby, that you and your team had a lot to do with it.

Within the last section of this book "Ready, Set, Go!", we will cover a practical example of how to bring this collaboration and idea sharing to life through Design Thinking. I will use the five stages of Design Thinking according to the Hasso-Plattner Institute of Design at Stanford (d.school) as a reference: Empathize, Define, Ideate, Prototype and Test. Stay tuned!

THE EMPLOYEE JOURNEY

Let's start with the concept of journey mapping. This is one of the most useful UX tools since it can provide a holistic view of how a person is experiencing different moments that can be delightful or frustrating. In order to build your journey you always need some key elements: a person (also known as 'persona' which we will address shortly to keep up with the human-centered approach!), situations, scenarios or phases that this person will experience, expectations, pain points (the emotional effect, frustration, anger, sadness, you name it) and wow moments (delight, happiness, pleasant surprises, etc). When done right, we can assess those pain points and find solutions or improvements. We might think we've got it easy if we identify lots of positive feelings and delight, but the truth is they might be harder to sustain in the long run and keeping or renewing the wow factor can become challenging.

Think about your current or last employee experience. I'm sure you can identify the key moments of your journey: when you got your first phone call, the first interview, your onboarding (or lack thereof), learning opportunities, performance management, even your decision to leave the organization and how it was handled. I'm sure you've got a lot of feelings around that experience, and you can easily identify what made you feel happy, optimistic, disappointed, angry, sad, and so on. Off the back of those feelings and moments, there's a massive ground for HR to do better (and even for yourself to do better in the future when facing certain phases).

PERSONA

Carl Gustav Jung, the Swiss psychiatrist, introduced the concept of archetypes as models of people, personality traits and behaviors. He identified four major archetypes (but with the caveat that there was not a limited number of archetypes!).The first one is the persona, which is the outward or social personality we show to others; the second one is the anima (female image in the male psyche) or animus (male image in the female psyche) and the roles each gender plays in the collective mind; the third one is the shadow that represents our darker side and the way we've adapted it to norms or expectations; and the fourth one is the self, which is the union of our personality as a whole. As interesting as this is (for me), we'll move on with this piece of introductory psychology information and go back to the experience.

When you're working with Design Thinking, you might hear people talk about how the personas are archetypes (to be honest Mr. Jung was spot on!). The term "persona" is used as the starting point and it refers to the user, customer or employee. This person exists within a particular situation or organization, and will be the center of any initiatives you will build, the beneficiary of your creative solution. It's not just about naming a person and identifying their age and gender; it goes way beyond that. Persona is all about knowing them enough to understand what they need and how you can empathize with them and offer solutions that are relevant and desirable.

This is the perfect chance to understand what they are all about: their biography, demographics, personality traits, what they love, what they don't love, their network. The more you know about them, the better.

I will (super-ultra-mega) oversimplify an example just for illustrative purposes. Let's say you would like to develop a new app for your customers (regardless of the industry you're in). As you know from life, it's impossible to make everyone happy and get them to be delighted, but you can certainly delight most of them. You would have to find out what would be the middle ground between someone who loves apps and is tech savvy and the person who hates smartphones and still dreams about their Nokia. Finding the middle ground can be tough, but the road becomes easier when we let emotions in and start finding out what people love (and of course, what they love to hate). You might find that both love sharing with others and love dogs; and that they hate things that take time and are not straightforward. These two things are already giving you a hint of what they want and what would work for them: easy to use, allows you to share and get feedback (plus... throwing in a dog or two in the look & feel won't hurt anyone! - Renzo, I'm joking don't choke!)

The traditional Design Thinking approach would have you create more than one persona based on the most common customer/employee types. You would also have real data about their preferences off the back of customer research or market research because the more real the information you have to work with the better the results. This will allow you to focus on the outcomes and the best experience your personas can have.

For our employee journey, I want to introduce you to Catherine MacLean, our "designated fictional persona" who will go through the phases and situations. Below you will find relevant information about her in a very Design Thinking/ CX/EX way: a mini biography, personality traits, her age, what a day in her life looks like and what she loves and hates.

CATHERiNE MACLEAN

MiNi BiO:

Catherine, oldest of three sisters, born in the country but moved to the city to go to college and decided to stay. She is a marketing professional, with six years of experience in retail and the Food and Beverage Industry

* **AGE:** 33 (but feels forever 21)
* **A DAY iN HER LiFE:**

Wakes up at 6 am to get her morning run, then gets ready to get to work at 8 am to deal with suppliers and designers. Gets home around 8 pm to have dinner with her significant other and feeds Ghost the stray cat (soon to be hers!). Gets a bit of TV binge in when possible or Yoga if it's a Tuesday or a Thursday.

Introvert	Extrovert
Rational	Emotional
Evasive	Direct
Impatient	Patient
People Oriented	Task Oriented

* LOVES:

* Her family and friends
* Instagram
* Animals, but cats and llamas are her favorite (has a thing for Llamas since her trip to Peru)
* Keeping up with the latest trends in fashion
* Getting recognized by a job well done
* Keeping up with the Kardashians' and "Love Island"
* Running in the mornings
* Year-end parties

* HATES:

* Being called Cathy
* Whatsapp and Facebook
* Her morning commute, especially when people stand on the left when they know better!
* People who are disrespectful
* Bad customer service and waiting (in general)
* Long hours at work
* Meetings that could have been an email
* Human Resources and their bullsh*t

OUR PERSONA'S NETWORK

To make sure I don't lose you during Catherine's experience, I want to introduce you to her network at the place where she works (Very likely that you will need to look at this again when we start with Catherine's journey. You can thank Fe Martinez, my editor, for this brilliant idea that I certainly didn't think of!)

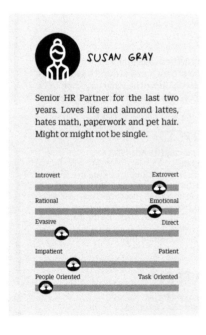

SUSAN GRAY

Senior HR Partner for the last two years. Loves life and almond lattes, hates math, paperwork and pet hair. Might or might not be single.

Introvert	Extrovert
Rational	Emotional
Evasive	Direct
Impatient	Patient
People Oriented	Task Oriented

THOMAS BAKE

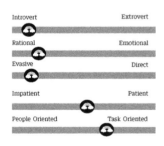

HR Partner, joined Company A six months ago. Ended up in HR by chance, would really like to move to a different department. Happily married, has one bonsai.

Introvert	Extrovert
Rational	Emotional
Evasive	Direct
Impatient	Patient
People Oriented	Task Oriented

JAMES MCLAUGHLIN

CEO for Company A since 2010. Likes being called J-Mac. Has one daughter and is married to his high school sweetheart. Says he's people oriented but actually would rather focus on getting things done.

Introvert — Extrovert
Rational — Emotional
Evasive — Direct
Impatient — Patient
People Oriented — Task Oriented

ADAM DRUITZ

Marketing Director, joined the company seven years ago. Loves a good beer, his two kids and his dog. Hates small talk and other people's kids, not a fan of explaining things (Especially to HR)

Introvert — Extrovert
Rational — Emotional
Evasive — Direct
Impatient — Patient
People Oriented — Task Oriented

WILMER SANTOS

Systems Analyst by day, blood elf by night. Loves video games and a good chat. His favorite phrase is: "Have you turned it off and on again?". Dislikes pedantic people and 9-5 hours (but has a mortgage to pay)

Introvert — Extrovert
Rational — Emotional
Evasive — Direct
Impatient — Patient
People Oriented — Task Oriented

KATRINA KUROWSKA

Marketing Analyst, been here for a year and it's her first job. She's one of Catherine's direct reports (the kids). Loves dancing and photography. Hates excel spreadsheets and Nutella (Eww, palm oil). Has a dark sense of humor people wouldn't expect. Lives with Chris (the love of her life)

Introvert — Extrovert
Rational — Emotional
Evasive — Direct
Impatient — Patient
People Oriented — Task Oriented

SAM HUNT

Marketing Analyst, specialize in Marketing because his love of brands (especially Coca-Cola), also Catherine's direct report. Been at Company A for a year and a half. Considers himself an overachiever, and is sure he is the perfect example of "Forever alone" when it comes to love.

Introvert	Extrovert
Rational	Emotional
Evasive	Direct
Impatient	Patient
People Oriented	Task Oriented

RAMONA YI

Star PA, has more years of service than the CEO within Company A and knows how everything works. Tries to like everyone but only loves her three kids. Has a low tolerance and zero time for bullsh*t. She's an early riser, but you won't find her around the office after 4pm. No Whatsapp. Ever.

Introvert	Extrovert
Rational	Emotional
Evasive	Direct
Impatient	Patient
People Oriented	Task Oriented

JEN SOUTHEAST

Marketing Senior Manager, one of Catherine's peers. Has been at Company A for five years. Eyeroll specialist, loves her morning coffee. Has two kids and no tolerance for pets. Not even dogs.

Introvert	Extrovert
Rational	Emotional
Evasive	Direct
Impatient	Patient
People Oriented	Task Oriented

ANTONIO INSIGNIA

Marketing Senior Manager, another one of Catherine's peers. Hates disagreements and conflicts. Loves lists and his cat Cesar. Divorced and active on Tinder. Not much of a sharer unless it's with Adam as they've got an open bromance going on.

Introvert	Extrovert
Rational	Emotional
Evasive	Direct
Impatient	Patient
People Oriented	Task Oriented

EMPLOYEE JOURNEY

In his article "Trends in employee maps" Mr. Tom Haaks (not Hanks) has identified and collated twenty different employee journeys that are presented in a series of drawings. The images go from traditional roads (which is the one I picked for this book) up to mountains, jungles and boat rides. The average number of phases included within the employee journey is 6.23. Some are basic three phase journeys of the employee's experience starting on the pre-onboarding, moving on to the onboarding and finishing with the offboarding. Others are more complex and include up to nine phases.

I want us to focus on six main phases for Catherine's employee journey, where I will include my colleagues' and my own two cents of experience on being your regular employee, resilient job seekers, consultants, HR professionals, project managers, finance professionals, among others. I'm also counting on you to bring up your own experience and insights, and write them down on the corresponding phase. Please see our chosen journey below:

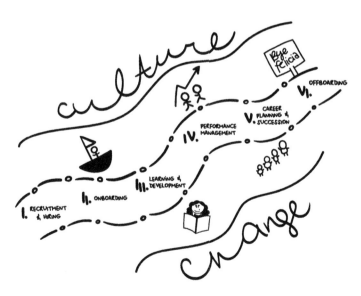

Even though we will focus on what's happening to Catherine (The good, the bad and the ugly), I will also take the chance to reflect a bit on the pain points that HR and the Business (non-HR areas) can experience during the same phases. Remember that these pain points are subjective, and normally have to do with what people feel, do, think and say about certain situations. Therefore, they are not wrong nor right. Addressing different people's pain points is a bit unorthodox, but will help because whether you are an employee, HR Professional or someone from the business side that works with HR, you will be able to relate. #Iteration2 of this book could have the whole shebang in detail (Employee, HR, Business). Baby steps, people!

For the HR perspective, I asked the HR Ninjas for help to get a quick gauge on their point of view of the challenges within the employee journey. I asked them which phase of the journey they find we struggle with the most / is the hardest for HR to get right. The small sample included 84 'HR Ninjas' who kindly gave their opinion as per the chart below.

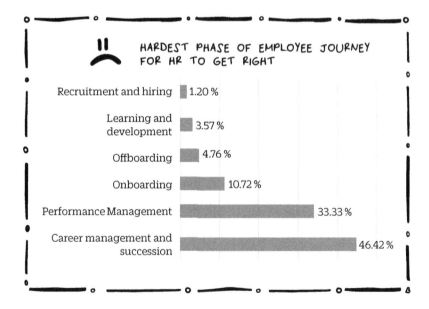

HARDEST PHASE OF EMPLOYEE JOURNEY FOR HR TO GET RIGHT

Phase	Percentage
Recruitment and hiring	1.20 %
Learning and development	3.57 %
Offboarding	4.76 %
Onboarding	10.72 %
Performance Management	33.33 %
Career management and succession	46.42 %

Career management and succession planning were the biggest winners (or losers?), followed by performance management and onboarding. There was little concern around offboarding and learning and development; and virtually no concern around recruitment and hiring (playing devil's advocate here...maybe because it's outsourced?). I think we struggle with most of them, but I was surprised that offboarding was not at the top of the list. Even though the offboarding process is in place in almost every organization, the data gathered there is likely to stay within an Excel document and never see the light of day again.

The business' pain points I've heard about the most tend to be related to the lack of support they get from HR and how HR is not a real strategic partner for them. They also get frustrated because we don't seem to understand the business or how the different areas operate and what they need. Plus, we take too long in simple tasks. As you can see, they're all very good friends of Mr. Hammonds. The other bit that rubs them off the wrong way is that HR doesn't have many indicators, evidence, data of the work that gets done and what works well for the business. If there are indicators in place, it might take a while for HR to produce a comprehensive and relevant one pager about them. HR on the other hand, always complains that the non-HR areas never have time and are never as engaged as they should be with people initiatives. They're also the ones to blame when things go wrong because "It's the managers' fault" (Rainbow, here is where I like to play devil's advocate and ask: Who is supposed to guide the managers? *Stares at HR*)

As the subtitle for this book hinted at ('Effective and collaborative HR throughout the employee journey', in case you forgot), we will cover the employee journey starting with the experience before joining the organization up to the day they leave (and beyond if HR is doing a good job!). This means understanding what happens in each phase, reflect on the pain points for HR, the business and the employee and some of the best practices I've seen or that my colleagues have kindly shared with me. After we've gone through the journey, you will find what I like to call "The heart of it all", which refers to organizational culture and change management. These two aspects are a major part of the employee experience because they are embedded across the whole journey and they can either break or make the journey. Culture is the essence of what the organization feels, behaves and thinks; and change is how it manages those feelings, behaviors and thoughts in a sustainable way. Regardless of our role, we must recognize the elements of the organizational culture we're a part of and make sure we gear up to manage change and embrace it.

BEFORE WE GET CRACKIN...

Catherine's experience will show the delights and pains of her journey within a company. If you're an HR professional or someone who's had the joy to experience an effective HR department, you'll probably think: "We do better than that". Kudos to you if you are, but unfortunately that's not the norm with HR. I might become your personal Mr. Hammonds because of this, but I know you will be a better sport than I was eleven years ago, and *know* that we can all do things even better.

Friendly reminder that this book is meant to be an illustrative and fun (fingers crossed!) approach to the employee journey, HR's role, culture, change and how to drive collaboration and creative solutions. So expect it not to be a detailed, process and policy heavy reading material. There are certainly things I've missed, and things I could have described better (#Iteration2). But if you're ok with that, let's move along!

Below you will find suggestions for further reading in case you'd like to stretch yourself further. They are all one Google or Amazon search away:

* Revolutionizing The Employee Experience: Four Ways To Use UX For EX.
Kate Rand for Forbes

* Time for an EX intervention?
Naina Dhingra, Jonathan Emmett and Mahin Samadani for McKinsey Organization Blog

* Design an Employee Experience that improves Business Performance
by Gallup

* Emotional Design: Why we love (or hate) everyday things
by Donald Norman

* Diseno de Experiencia de Empleado (EX): Un Mundo de Abundancia
by Isabel Loaldi

* Trends in employee maps
by Tom Haaks

* Five stages in the Design Thinking Process
by Rikke Friis Dam and Yu Siang Theo

* Archetypes and the Collective Unconscious
by Carl Gustav Jung

* Is Onboarding The New HR Secret For Company Success?
Interview by Bruce Rogers

* The Most In-Demand Hard and Soft Skills of 2020
by Bruce Anderson

* Your Company Needs a Process for Offboarding Employees Gracefully by David Sturt

* Organizational Culture and Cultural Change
by The Chartered Institute of Personnel and Development

* Who Says Elephants Can + Dance
by Lou Gerstner

* Six Components of a Great Corporate Culture
by John Coleman

* Making Change Work While The Work Keeps Changing
by IBM

* Don + Just Tell Employees Organizational Changes Are Coming Explain Why by Morgan Galbraith

* Impact : 21st Century Change Management, Behavioral Science, Digital Transformation and the Future of Work
by Paul Gibbons

* The Life-Changing Magic of Not Giving a F**k
by Sarah Knight (Not EX/UX related, but Personal Experience (PX) related!)

* 12 Rules for Life : An Antidote to Chaos
by Jordan B. Peterson (Same as above!)

RECRUITMENT & HIRING

Catherine's earned her Marketing stripes for the past years in Retail and the Food and Beverage industry, but now she's looking for something new after two and a half years in the same organization. She's at work but she's got some time to do a quick search (yes, yes, she is looking for a new job during her work hours - You've probably done/will do the same at some point so don't judge!). Within ten minutes, she's already found five positions she likes. There's one with particularly bright colors and a lovely summary of the organization's values (Company A), another one with sleek black and white design (Company B), and the other three (Companies C, D and E) are pretty plain but state they're paying between 10-15K above what she gets today. Companies A, B and E have a "Easy Apply" option so just with a simple click, she's applied to the three of them. Companies C and D redirect to the organization's website for her to fill in her data within their own formatting and ask for a cover letter (*yawn*). Not today.

Couple of weeks go by and Company A has emailed her to ask her availability for an interview, same with Company E except they decided to call her instead of emailing and said they'll be in touch shortly to set up a meeting. Company B has said nothing (they did state in the job ad they were expecting a high volume of applicants).

She goes to Company A's interview, signs in at reception through an iPad and waits about 25 minutes after the agreed time for the interview (Yes, the interviewers are LATE. Those bastards, she needs to get back to work from her "doctor's appointment"). Once the interviewers are there, they do apologize for the delay but she's still not happy about it, but she smiles because she wants the job. She has also liked the whole office vibe, the casual dress code, and the iPad sign-up shenanigans. Interviewers are actually quite nice, but some of their questions are a bit cliché (Where do you see yourself in five years? What are your strengths/weaknesses? What do you have to offer for this position?). They mention there is another round of interviews happening, this time with the Director of their area so HR will be in touch.

Company E on the other hand, invited her to an assessment center with six other candidates to do some group dynamics for two hours, possibly to measure her leadership and collaboration skills. She was asked to introduce herself and mention why she chose to apply there. They did start and finish on time so she'll be at work right after her "train cancellation". She feels she's done a good job at the group tasks but hates it when people operate at a slower pace (which they definitely did, she can't believe she's up against those guys for the role!). Cat's defo in the bag. Week and a half later she gets an email from some Karen gal from HR saying that unfortunately they were moving forward with someone else, no further reasons. Cat was defo not in the bag, and one of those other five guys will now get 15K more than she does now. F*ck them.

To lift up her spirit, someone from HR calls her from Company A day after her initial interview. He says the Director would love to meet her ASAP because they want to move quite quickly with this position. Yay! Off she goes to that happy, happy reception and signs up on her own on the iPad because she knows the deal now. Director is absolutely adorable, completely different from that assh*le Ruth she is currently reporting to. Come on mate, give her a chance! Before she leaves the meeting room he says he doesn't normally do this...but he's loved her experience and thinks she's a good fit so wants her to join. HR will be in touch. She's over the moon!

HR indeed gets in touch and sends her an email with the title "Welcome to the team, Catherine!". Attached is the offer with the economical proposal and the extra benefits. She's being asked to confirm her starting date, her ID and some other bits and bobs that she already has at hand. They've also offered to share some reading materials before her onboarding. She's accepted the offer! She speaks to Ruth, and to her surprise she was not a complete assh*le.

Randomly she gets a phone call. It's Company B asking to meet for informal coffee. Are they kidding?! Three months after she applied for the role?! **Bye Felicia**.

CATHERINE S EXPERIENCE

I'm pretty sure you can pinpoint Catherine's experience and its moments of Pain & Delight (P&D) during the Recruitment and Hiring process from the three different companies, some of them:

PAIN POINTS

* **COVER LETTER REQUESTS:** Nope. Ain't nobody got time for that. Even though the roles might have been interesting, the additional effort makes it annoying (Yes, we are all lazy by nature!)

* **CLICHÉ QUESTIONS:** Especially the ones around Strengths and Weaknesses, also annoying

* **GOING THROUGH THE ASSESSMENT CENTER WITH PEOPLE WHO WERE NOT AS UP TO SPEED AS SHE WAS HAS BEEN FRUSTRATING.** This one particularly intensifies when she gets rejected (her ego's got a bubu!), especially because, at least in her mind, she had this in the bag. Not to mention she wasted her time for nothing

* **WAITING 25 MINUTES FOR COMPANY A'S INTERVIEWERS**. Big no no, especially with her low tolerance for waiting

* **GETTING GHOSTED BY COMPANY B**...no comments

DELIGHTS

* **EASY APPLY FUNCTION WITHIN LINKEDIN IS SUCH A GREAT THING!**

* **SHE'S A FAN OF GADGETS AND TECHNOLOGY,** so iPad signing-in system was great for her

* **BEING TOLD BY THE DIRECTOR STRAIGHT AFTER THE INTERVIEW THAT SHE'S THE ONE THEY WANT FOR THE ROLE** (Now that cat was in the bag!)

* **BYE FELICIA'ING COMPANY B BECAUSE SHE'S ALREADY GOT COMPANY A.** The satisfaction of politely saying "No, thank you" when you actually mean "Suck it!"

THINK ABOUT YOUR OWN EXPERIENCE AT THIS PHASE OF THE EMPLOYEE JOURNEY, WHAT WERE YOUR P&DS?

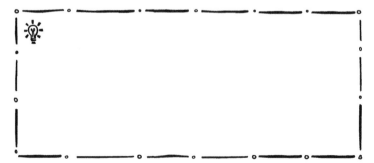

BUSINESS PAIN POINTS - RECRUITMENT & HIRING

When you are in an area that is not HR, but you're still part of the 'recruiting & hiring chain' you will likely be asked to invest time in the process (whether you like it or not, it's not HR's sole responsibility to get you your dream candidate!). Most of the time, I've heard people from those other areas say they're struggling with HR during the recruitment process (and through other processes). Their main pain points are always around three topics:

One of them is because HR has not provided any guidance on how to do a competency-based interview, or even suggest general questions to manage and interview. Managers are left on their own and despite their experience, it can be a source of anxiety for them. The second one is the availability factor. No one has all the availability in the world to interview all the people they want, and whenever they want. Finally, finding the right candidate can take time, which for business-speakers translates into: "HR takes ageeeeeeeeeeees to find decent candidates," plus while they look for the one they can send the wrong people for interviews with the hiring manager. This is, understandably, a waste of productive hours.

HR PAIN POINTS - RECRUITMENT & HIRING

Hiring managers from the business (non-HR areas) always say they have no time to attend HR trainings in general, let alone interview skills trainings. Worst is that when they do attend, they tend to give terrible feedback about it (Boohoo, Rainbow).

When hiring managers interview people, they tend not to give objective and real answers on why they're saying no to a candidate. They seem to make decisions based on their "gut" rather than real, unbiassed reasons. Good candidates are put forward just for them to say it's a no in a vague email. This means HR can't go back to the candidate with valid feedback.

ADDRESSiNG THE PAiN POiNTS - RECRUiTMENT & HiRiNG

HR has a lot to do with addressing the pain points and keeping the delights. Even in the case that your Recruitment and Hiring process is outsourced, you need to set the rules and the "vibe" your experience will have.

The key is finding the right approach to get this done when on one hand the business "has no time for HR bullsh*t" and on the other hand candidates in the job hunt will certainly share their good, bad and ugly experiences with the world.

Stating that you get a high volume of CVs (*eyeroll*) is a pretty lame excuse to not put in the effort to get back to the candidates that are not a match. They're not expecting a break-up letter, just a thank you for your interest. Pretty easy to automate emails with a Macros on Excel.

When rejecting a candidate after an interview or assessment, please be kind and provide constructive feedback. You might say as an HR person "Someone from the Business did the interview, so I don't really know what to say to the candidate". Guess what, Rainbow? -It's your responsibility to get proper feedback from the business and share it with the candidate (That is, if you want to leave a good impression of your organization)

HR can and should train hiring managers on interviewing skills (if you are a hiring manager, you're entitled to get support from HR to nail interviews!). This is done to ensure consistency and fairness in the recruitment and selection process. As HR, you can give guidance or useful templates to your interviewers regardless of their seniority. It could be a one-pager with straightforward formatting around the key questions, space for notes, and (very important) guidance on how to give the feedback to HR after the interviews / assessments / sessions.

Don't take AGES to get back to candidates that have applied for a job. Whether it is a yes or a no, do it timely (No more than two weeks). Don't ghost them. When sending the offer to the candidate, state that you will be there to answer any questions they might have (Might sounds obvious, but people do like to hear/read this even if they don't have immediate questions). HR is the first point of contact for candidates, so make sure you are making their experience a good one from the start.

Another key point is getting your indicators rolling, and this will apply to all phases of the journey (and to Culture and Change as well). Ideally, these are set by HR and shared with the rest of the business' leaders so they're in the loop of how you're measuring HR's work (Plus, they could have some ideas on this as well...#SharingIsCaring)

For Recruitment and Hiring, these are some indicators you might want to consider:

• What are your sourcing channels? What percentage of candidates come from which one? How effective are the channels?

• What's the average time to hire someone? (From first contact to accepting the offer)

• How many interviews, assessment centers or other recruitment & selection activities do you deliver per month/year? (This might be different per business area)

- How many people you interview per month/year? How many of those get a job offer? And how many accept the offer?

- How much does it cost to recruit and hire a candidate?

- How many new joiners are happy with the recruitment and hiring process?

- Hiring manager's satisfaction with the process and new hire

And let's not forget...

- What are your unsuccessful candidates saying about the recruitment process? (This information is key to getting improvement opportunities)

PHASE II
ONBOARDING

Catherine is getting ready to start her new job at Company A. Lucky for her, her commute will be 20 minutes shorter than her previous one. She gets to the office, her office. She won't need to sign-up on the iPad again because she's been told to wait by the "New Joiner" sign at reception and wait for Susan from HR at 9am for breakfast and networking. She's already read a bit about Company A on the pre-onboarding materials they sent her right after she signed the job offer. She knows about it's mission, vision and values, the different business areas, among other things.

Susan is there at five to 9am and starts greeting everyone, she seems quite nice and chipper. She's introducing herself to all those who have arrived and letting everyone know that she'll be taking them to the meeting room for some breakfast and the activities will start at 9:15am.

To Catherine's surprise the meeting room actually looks like a fancy ass living room with beautiful sofas and a huge screen. There's a round table in the middle with coffee, tea and milk...but behold the big tray with pastries, yay sugar rush! But wait...there's also fruit, that's a better choice. But maybe just one cream filled pastry won't hurt after that.

She starts talking to the guy on her right who has joined the Finance team from a big four company. Figures, as he seems out of his element with casualwear, must be all those years he spent wearing a suit every day.

Lucky for her, that's not one of her problems.

It's 9:15am and Susan is giving those who are late a chance to get there. It's 9:30am and they're starting, she introduces her co-facilitator, Thomas (who looks like he needs a coffee and is definitely not as chipper as Susan). She asks the new joiners to introduce themselves by stating their names, previous company they worked for, something they love and something they don't like.

Once they finish with 25 introductions, they move onto the mission, vision and values which is pretty much the same as what she read last night. Their purpose is linked to giving the best experience they can to clients. And their values are based on passion, accountability, commitment to clients (both internal and external), innovation and honesty. They move along to the organizational chart but unfortunately it only has names, no pictures. They're all asked to locate who their head of area is and to get into smaller groups with those who are in the same area as them. After that, they've got an hour assigned with the IT crowd who walk in carrying 25 laptops and chargers and start handing them over to each newbie. "Everything is pretty straightforward to set up, but let us know if you have any questions. I'm John Kant, K-A-N-T like the philosopher, and this is my mate Wilmer Santos, that's W-I-L-M-E-R / S-A-N-T-O-S." Someone asks them to write their names on the board to make it easier. They comply, but they're not exactly excited about it. It's obvious that they want to get out ASAP. Plus, they had taken the time to spell out their names.

Just like that it's 4pm, and Thomas starts wrapping up saying that he hopes they enjoyed the day. But before their managers come pick them up, the CEO James McLaughlin (Or J-Mac as they introduced him) comes in for a brief five-minute window to say hi and wish them the best of luck on their journey with Company A. He takes time to make eye contact with each and every single joiner. He suggests they invest time in getting to know people, and to get ready to be flexible because that's how they roll.

Adam, her director is nowhere to be found and suddenly she feels like the odd kid at school whose parent is late to pick her up. Finally, Adam shows up fifteen minutes late "Sorry meetings tend to run longer all the time here." Good thing is he's brought her a coffee and sits next to her explaining that tomorrow she can meet the team in the morning. "See you at 9am tomorrow, go home, have a nice dinner and get some sleep. We need you well-rested for tomorrow."

Her second day comes along and Adam huddles the team up at 9:45am instead of 9am (Whatever people!). It certainly looks like they were there in way before 9am anyway... He introduces her to Sam and Katrina (who are her direct reports, and will be known as "the kids" going forward); Jen and Antonio (her peers, the ones that were late to interview her as you may recall) and their respective direct reports whose names she didn't quite catch. She feels awkward to ask again. She spends her second day texting her ex colleagues and friends and setting up her email account and sorting her access to shared folders. She's had to contact Wilmer Santos (S-A-N-T-O-S) twice for help. He's been surprisingly helpful. It's 6pm and she notices nobody is any close to leaving the building, but she will because she's got nothing urgent and Ghost the cat is waiting for her at home.

First week and second week go by uneventfully, everybody seems to be really busy and she hasn't gotten any one-to-one time with Adam until the week after. She's not really sure what she needs to do so she sets some time with the kids every morning for an hour so they get her up to speed. Her initial gut feeling about them being entitled little pricks was way off. They're very bright, chatty and seem to be keen to learn from her (Sam a bit more than Katrina, but they're both lovely).

At the end of the first month she gets an email from her friendly HR Senior Partner, Susan Gray, who is just checking in to say hi and to see how she's getting on.

She is great! Ah...she's also sent a link with a satisfaction survey...that's what she really wanted.

Just like that, Catherine has been in the company for almost a year and she hasn't seen much of the other 24 new joiners in her cohort. She's seen Susan again a couple of times and had small talk but the excitement from day one has definitely washed off. She's also seen Thomas, who seems to not be great with eye contact or the word "Hello". Whatever. She's also learned a great deal on how things are done by snooping around her departments' shared folders. She knows she's walked into a place with certainly lots of passion but not much accountability. The documents are all over the place, there's no track on who did what, not many processes in place. She's suggested to do a Marie Kondo on their shared folders to her peers, and their answer was: "We'll get to that later, let's just get over this week first!"

She's also made a friend in a high place, Ramona, the CEO's personal assistant. Ramona has been at Company A longer than the CEO and most of the other C-Suiters. She's been incredibly helpful with the "who is who", but also with how things are done in this place. One thing is certain: she doesn't like her line manager Adam that much.

CATHERINE'S EXPERIENCE

PAIN POINTS

* **AGAIN WITH TIME MANAGEMENT AND BEING LATE PEOPLE!** Staaaaphhhh (It's her persona's peeve, and it seems like their norm)

* **FEELING LOST DURING THE FIRST MONTH, WHICH ALSO IMPACTS HER ABILITY TO GET THINGS DONE** (which is something she likes, remember she loves getting recognized for a job well done. And she can't do a good job unless she knows what she has to do, and what is the expectation of that)

* **LIMITED AVAILABILITY FROM HER DIRECTOR TO GUIDE HER AND HER PEERS.** I'm sure we can share the frustration

* **NOT HAVING A REAL CONTACT AT HR.** It doesn't feel like she can reach out to them for help. Susan was lovely on day one, and nice at the end of the first month with her email but that was about it. Don't even get her started on Thomas the no-eye-contact-no-hello mister...

DELiGHTS

* **THE FACT THAT HR ORGANIZED FOR J-MAC TO COME IN WAS GREAT**, and he even wishing them best of luck in their journey with Company A

* **SUSAN'S PERSONALIZED EMAIL TO CHECK IN ON HER**, that's a first in her work experience! (Even though it came with the survey it was nice of her)

* **HER DIRECT REPORTS SEEM TO BE NICER THAN WHAT SHE THOUGHT INITIALLY.** Go team!

* **WILMER SANTOS' HELPFULNESS.** Didn't expect that from the IT crowd

THINK ABOUT YOUR OWN EXPERIENCE AT THIS PHASE OF THE EMPLOYEE JOURNEY, WHAT WERE YOUR P&Ds?

BUSINESS PAIN POINTS - ONBOARDING

Even though the organizational onboarding is done on the first day and it responds to the basic need of new joiners to know the company, the business tends to feel like HR should do more of something during the first week, and even the first months.

When a new joiner comes in, there's a lot of introducing to the team and babysitting to do for which (again) they don't have time for. Can't HR keep them for a month or two and send them back when they know everything about the business? Wait...they can't, because HR people don't know the business! (*eyeroll*)

HR PAIN POINTS - ONBOARDING

It's safe to say that HR has a lot of processes in their hands, and therefore they feel they don't have enough bandwidth to keep up with all the new joiners and satisfy the business in having a longer, more significant onboarding process. The responsibility of onboarding people falls only within the HR bucket (I know, I know... it's like we're the laundry basket!)

New joiners often forget to fill in satisfaction surveys, especially if they're sent after the session. There is a challenge to get data on this phase and the general feeling is this happens with anything where we depend on others to do.

ADDRESSING THE PAIN POINTS - ONBOARDING

First impressions are important to any relationship, and the work relationship might have started with the interviews, but you seal the deal with the onboarding. People should arrive to the first session already knowing a bit about the organization, the mission, vision and values or behaviors and HR is definitely in charge of that.

The onboarding can't be just about the organization's mission, vision and values. Teach the new joiners about the business your organization is in. Whether they come from other industries or roles, they need to know the basics of how your business operates. Let's say you're in Retail, you need to explain the basics of how the business works. Talk to them about the breakdown cost of a T-Shirt sold by your brand (what percentage of the cost goes to material and fabrics costs, to the worker that made the T-Shirt, the profit to the brand, to the intermediary, to retail, overhead costs, transport costs, etc.)

In my experience, involving non-HR people to deliver the onboarding session and support the onboarding process the first six months is part of that strategic HR that the business wants to see. The first day can be a winning trick with this combination of HR + Non-HR because it shows collaboration throughout the organization and can be a motivator for the new joiners to help HR in the future. The people leading the onboarding need to be great at interpersonal skills, since they are the first point of contact with the company. Assigning an HR Representative for each cohort of new joiners is key.

Seeing the onboarding as a six-month process rather than an induction day is key (it also happens to be the average time for an employee to perform!). There needs to be a plan for those six months. Checking in only after the first month can only do so much. Remember, relationships are about quality but frequency doesn't hurt at all. Make sure to contact the cohort as a group just to check-in twice the first month, and monthly during the following five months.

HR should guide the different areas so they can build their own onboarding, which can help the new joiners transition easily into their roles. For this to happen, the area onboarding needs to include the specifics about the team's ways of working, systems that they use, high level understanding of the different sub-teams within the areas and their pictures. It might be a b*tch to update with potential leavers/movers, but it's completely worth it. They also need to measure that on their own and HR can help setting those indicators. Fun fact: Christian Harpelund states that companies with a structured and standardized onboarding processes experience 54% higher productivity from new employees, they're twice as engaged and their average time to performance is 6,2 months.

Some indicators you can use for the onboarding phase are:

- If you send pre-onboarding materials, establish a percentage of how many new joiners have read them

- New hire satisfaction with the onboarding (how useful they found the first day session, would they recommend the session, do they feel prepared, etc.)

- Line manager's satisfaction with the onboarding process

- Time to productivity (Line managers are also a useful reference for this one, so is self-perception)

- Your retention rate and average time that an employee stays in the organization can be a useful indicator of the onboarding effectiveness

- Lastly, what I will call #UXingTheSh*tOutofEXAlert. You will get tired of reading this in the next phases as well, but it's proven that repetition is a good learning mechanism! Lucky for you I will not get tired of repeating it so it sticks with you: Qualitative feedback and fresh ideas will be a big part of your overall indicators, go get 'em Tiger! Talk to the employees, ask the right questions at the right time (meaning, don't wait two/three weeks to ask for it, do it ASAP).

For example, right after the very first onboarding session, gather real-time feedback (print-out surveys -make them small to be environmental friendly!-, board with questions and happy faces or stars to rate each question, lots of post-its for suggestions, etc.) You will also need feedback of the overall process (this is assuming you will go for it as a process rather than an induction day). If you get ideas that are feasible and desirable don't take long to put them in action. And as soon as you put them in action, make sure to give them the proper recognition for their contribution and you've hit the jackpot at the end of the rainbow!

We will find out more on this topic in the last section of the book so stay tuned!

PHASE III
LEARNiNG & DEVELOPMENT (L&D)

Catherine has successfully passed her probation period, and she was not wrong about Adam (her area's director and line manager). He seems to be way better than Ruth (old boss), although he's a bit of a micromanager but she can handle that for now. Catherine has noticed that her peers are the same with their teams. This must be an organizational culture trait...that and having no respect for people's time when they show up late for meetings.

The micromanagement bit has been affecting her way of working as well because she's been quite hands on with her team (Sam and Katrina) and their interactions with suppliers and accounts payable. Especially since the Tech and Procurement area implemented a new system for Purchase Orders last month. She's gotten at least 200 emails (and counting!) from suppliers, accounts payable and the kids. This whole drama is happening because they don't know how to use the new system properly, as it was a "learn as you go" type of change; and also because instead of talking this through face-to-face, they keep firing emails! To be fair, they just got some communications that this change was happening and that they needed the list of their top 50 suppliers and their details, which Sam had sent as soon as they asked for the information. Sam forwarded a one pager PDF with some screens that seemed to be the new process but they weren't very clear. In her experience, this was a very crappy way of handling changes. They needed to learn about it and understand it, but both Sam and Katrina were just confused and frustrated with the whole thing and said a couple of times "Let's just go back to the other system, it worked better anyway".

Catherine emails Susan (her HR contact) about any courses coming her or her team's way to get to know the system's functionalities better, it must be a very straightforward thing to understand as it's just raising Purchase Orders and following up on receiving the goods and paying suppliers. She's also keen to help her team with some soft skills training but doesn't know how exactly to go about it (effective communication and having difficult conversations would be so handy now!). Susan replied saying that it's great they want to get some training rolling, and that she should start by browsing the company's intranet because they've got lots of resources available on the new system and soft skills related topics. She ends the email with a "Ping me on Skype if you need more info. Happy to help! XOXO". Wtf? She just directed me to a website? Is that all she can do?

The website is absolutely lovely, wonderfully designed, very attractive and colorful. Maybe she was too quick to judge? She starts navigating and indeed there is a sh*tload of information, a bit much to be honest, so she doesn't know where to start. She decides to leave it for another day.

Catherine starts thinking about when was the last time she had a face-to-face training session at Company A. Must have been during the onboarding, on day one. That can't be right...actually, it is. That's simply wrong. Before being one of those annoying people, she decides to be proactive so she deep dives into her emails and searches for the word "training" (Which is the "ugly" word for Learning & Development or L&D). She finds a couple of communications from HR that she clearly missed and left unread, one was even in the trash folder. Apparently, there was this "Learning & Development Festival" happening two months ago. Sh*t she missed it. Ahhh that's why there were so many balloons around the meeting room areas. Some of the offerings for training were: yoga, hot yoga, goat yoga (How many yogas can you offer?!), time management (Jesus take the wheel, please tell me this one is mandatory for these people!), effective communications (might work for the team?), leadership and performance management assessments (should have signed up for those for the sake of the kids!).

She's told Adam that she's more than happy to put a process in place for the area, to make sure they're getting the sessions they need for development on a personal and professional level. She's done this before and really enjoys sharing what she knows. She's even offered to kick-off this for the whole team with a couple of sessions on understanding customers (both internal and external) and new ways of learning through Google Analytics. The answer she got?: "Let HR do it, go get your reports ready for today's meeting!" So much for living the values of innovation and passion...

CATHERINE'S EXPERIENCE

PAIN POINTS

* **ON A PERSONAL NOTE, SHE'S DISAPPOINTED BECAUSE SHE'S GOT ACCOUNTABILITY ON HER TEAM MISSING OUT ON THE SESSIONS.** And that she missed them as well (especially around Performance Management which is just around the corner and she's still oh so relatively new to the organization). This has activated her Fear Of Missing Out (or FOMO), which may or may not lead to her paying more attention to HR Communications (It's still HR's fault anyway...)

* **SUSAN FROM HR TELLING TO TO "PING" HER ON SKYPE IF SHE NEEDS ANYTHING...** Might be the right words and tone to use with the approachable XOXO, but that doesn't get her results. She was expecting more support and they simply sent her a website

* **TOO MUCH INFORMATION IS OVERWHELMING,** which is exactly why she didn't pursue the research any further for training

materials or sessions

* **FRUSTRATION FOR NOT BEING ABLE TO SHARE HER KNOWLEDGE WITH THE TEAM, OR HELP THE AREA LEARN.** Why isn't Adam walking the talk of the organizational values anyway?

DELiGHTS

* **LOVELY COMMS, LOVELY WEBSITES, COLORFUL BALLOONS.** They all looked great and charming. But there's no real delight on missing out (FOMO is real!)

THINK ABOUT YOUR OWN EXPERIENCE AT THIS PHASE OF THE EMPLOYEE JOURNEY, WHAT WERE YOUR P&DS?

BUSINESS PAIN POINTS - L&D

The different areas normally have lots of internal processes that are not documented or sorted in an accessible place, so this is definitely a big pain point in general when it comes to knowledge sharing and training. "This is *exactly* what HR should be helping us with!"

Timing also plays a role in the non-HR areas' pain points. It would seem that HR schedules their events (like this alleged festival) without checking in with the different areas and agree on a date that can work for most. "Nobody can do it when we can get the speakers in". Boohoo, yet again.

HR PAIN POINTS - L&D

Let's face it, HR spends a lot of time drafting and designing attractive websites and communications and they are still left unread, unattended, even deleted. When this is the case, attendance on L&D initiatives tends to be low and HR's morale gets a hit. Too many resources invested for such a small return. There is a lot of organization behind training sessions (meeting room bookings, call with the trainers, buying materials, the list is quite long). But this effort is not seen by the attendees.

When planning L&D topics, "there's no time" to do a formal and detailed Training Needs Analysis (TNA) on what needs to be learned by whom, or what the expected outcomes are. This intensified by the fact that your audience is unsure of what they should be learning, let alone what they want. HR is officially annoyed by this, and takes the easy route: "Let's offer time management training session because everybody needs that, right?"

ADDRESSING THE PAIN POINTS - L&D

HR, as the strategic partner it should be, needs to joint by the hip to the business. It's time for....#UXingTheSh*tOutofEXAlert. Talk_to_people.

Make sure you agree with the leaders of the different areas on the dates and times. For example, don't even bother trying to get the Finance area involved during the month-end. Or the IT area when they're deploying updates to a system...let alone implementing one!
Trainings' topics need to respond to real employee needs within the workplace (and sometimes even outside of it to fluff up the "work/life balance", or the hype of "goat yoga").

Mentoring and coaching are also a L&D initiatives that are overlooked by organizations, and they are relatively cheap to implement given that the resources are already there and more people than you would imagine are willing to share and participate. It has been proven that mentoring and coaching strengthen the relationships between different areas, roles and levels within the organizations, promote knowledge sharing and have a significant impact on employee engagement and performance. And the best part? You can mix both soft and hard skills. This is another jackpot hitter. Go get 'em!

Something similar happens with internal trainers (another case of underutilization!). This one is particularly interesting because it helps engaged people share their knowledge and develop others at the same time. Try mapping a quick excel with "Who knows what?". You will be surprised by the amount of talent and knowledge you can find in a group of people!

Did I mention I'm a fan of indicators? GET 'EM SORTED! They will help you ensure that the employees are acquiring the knowledge they need to perform their jobs, and that your effort is having results. For example, you could consider:

- Percentage of attendance to learning and development events

- Number of sessions proactively designed and offered by HR

- Number of ad hoc sessions requested by non-HR areas to be delivered

- What are the satisfaction surveys saying? (Was the course useful? Do they feel more competent/better equipped after the session? Would they recommend the session?)

- How many soft skills learning sessions have been delivered? What about hard skills?

- Compare the results of the hard skills/soft skills. Are they the same? One better than the other? Why is that?

- What percentage of each business area has benefited from learning and development sessions?

- Competency test results (passing/failing criteria)

- What's the average number of hours employees spend on learning and development yearly? (Useful if you break this so each non-HR area can see theirs)

- Number of internal trainers

- Number of mentors/coaches and percentage of satisfaction with the process

- Average training course cost

- Training catalogue with what is available on soft skills and hard skills for the organization

PHASE IV
PERFORMANCE MANAGEMENT

Catherine's getting ready for her Performance Management review with her Director. She got some comms from HR a couple of weeks ago with the link to the template she has to use for performance feedback. She did read the communications this time for two reasons: because it's her first formal performance feedback, and because she has to do it for Sam and Katrina, her direct reports.

The template seems pretty straightforward: There's a bucket for achievements, another for challenges and a small section with a square that says "Employee's final rating". It goes from 1 to 5 and she's sure it's that typical Gauss bell situation that looks like the snake that ate the elephant on Le Petit Prince. How did it go? 2.1% are at the lowest performing employees with 1 (basically kicking them out should be the next step); 13 point something percent are at number 2; a big chunk around 60% is within the "mediocre middle" with a 3; another 13 point something percent with a 4 doing good; and finally the last 2.1% with the golden children of the upper 5 rating (Does that even sum up to a 100%? God knows, she's got no calculator at hand. Plus, she's a marketing person, and only has two people to rate anyway). She's always been used to being a 4 herself, a couple of times a 5 because she's good at what she does. She's not really concerned about her rating, she's worried about doing a fair evaluation for the kids.

She reaches out to the sender of the HR communications (Who happens to be Thomas the no-eye-contact-no-hello mister). He says he can meet in ten minutes around the cafeteria. That was a pleasant surprise, how fast! He shows up with a couple of printouts (the PDF that was attached to the communications and the communications art within the email. Ugh... seriously?!) He hands her the document and explains how this will guide her through the process and that it's really straightforward. He suggests that she gets some individual time with her direct reports (No sh*t, Sherlock. She was thinking about doing a team feedback session and flashing their ratings on the screen). This needs to be done before the end of the month and document results in the system. There are some restrictions, like overpromising pay raises or promotions and some legal mumbo jumbo. "It's all in the Frequently asked questions on the last page, everything else is the first five pages, but do speak to Adam before doing anything to be safe." She starts browsing the printout... she admits to herself it's actually a pretty solid, interesting document that she will review carefully on the train home. Thomas is now ready to say bye and quickly asks if there's anything else she might need. She shakes her head and off he goes.

She sets time with Adam, because she wants to see how the big boss does it. They sit together and Adam has printed out the template and scribbled around it. There's one thing that calls her attention, there's a big 3 in the rating square. WTF?! A 3?! After all her hard work throughout the year? Adam better be objective as f*ck to justify that 3. She came prepared with her list of 10 solid achievements and 4 challenges and how she overcame every single one of them. Adam agrees but is not leaving any room for a rating change. Adam closes the meeting with: "I'm happy with you in the team, like I said on the day we met you are a great fit. The thing is... you haven't been here long enough to demonstrate you are consistently operating on a higher rating, Cathy. I'm sure next year will be a different story, I've got great expectations." She hates being called Cathy, and she hates that 3 rating. She wonders what Antonio and Jen got. Don't go there Catherine, step away from comparisons. Plus, they've been here forever so if that's the standard for a 4 they must have gotten it.

CATHERINE'S EXPERIENCE

PAIN POINTS

* **HER RATING. UGH. MEDIOCRE 3.** Even though a 3 rating within an organization falls within the "as expected", she's pissed

* **DESPITE HER ACHIEVEMENTS AND CHALLENGES, ADAM DOESN'T SEEM TO BE LEAVING ANY ROOM FOR DISCUSSION ON THE RATING.** This is a major ego-buster, and just like 95% of us, Catherine likes being told she's done a good job. "You've not been here long enough" keeps coming back to her because it's clearly unfair if time in the company is a criteria for performance

* **THOMAS' OBVIOUS SUGGESTION OF GETTING INDIVIDUAL SESSIONS WITH HER DIRECT REPORTS**

DELIGHTS

* **HAVING A QUICK RESPONSE FROM HR.** Yay us!

* **SOLID DOCUMENTATION FROM HR AND A STRAIGHTFORWARD DOCUMENT TO FILL IN.** The system is pretty friendly as well so this would not be a hassle

THINK ABOUT YOUR OWN EXPERIENCE AT THIS PHASE OF THE EMPLOYEE JOURNEY, WHAT WERE YOUR P&DS?

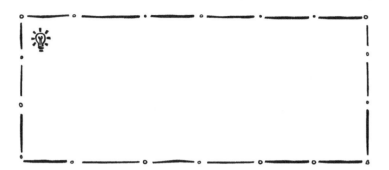

BUSINESS PAIN POINTS - PERFORMANCE MANAGEMENT

"HR has not explained the process to me, they just sent some comms out and they expect me to read it and know exactly what to do" (Well yes, Sunshine. We're expected to be adults and read on our own, but it's a fair point that we all love a good old 1-2-1 session).

Some managers might have it easier than others doing a fair and objective performance management session (especially if they've got experience a good set of soft skills). Other don't, and they need some help to get through this (Whether they like it or not, reaching to HR is actually a good call for this)

HR PAIN POINTS - PERFORMANCE MANAGEMENT

"Managers don't take enough time to review the documentation that is prepared for certain situations, and it feels as if the managers in the different areas need to be spoon-fed" #ReadYourEmail

"May we also remind you that we offered training sessions on performance management during the 'L&D Festival'?" (We know, we know...)

Deadlines for performance management reviews seem to be optional rather than mandatory for some managers, and HR becomes Henry Cavill on the Witcher, except we're hunting ratings and submissions instead of monsters. HR also happens to hear a lot of complaints about the process through the grapevine, but never any ideas of how to make it better and fair. This is another big opening for....#UXingTheSh*tOutofEXAlert

ADDRESSING THE PAIN POINTS - PERFORMANCE MANAGEMENT

The best type of feedback is the one that is continuous and doesn't depend on the year-end reviews that have to be submitted on the system. It's about the feedback culture and that can be driven by HR through the leaders of the different areas. The leaders of the organization set the expectation and the path, and they set how their direct reports will behave when evaluating their direct reports. It's all connected. HR needs to give them the skills, and again, the approach and timings need to be agreed upfront to ensure that managers attend any sessions that will give them the skills to face performance management.
Best practice is to also be transparent about ratings and how you achieve each rating. I've seen organizations send out communications around how they did as a whole, with the average of all the employees' ratings. How this information lands depends greatly on the level of maturity of the organization.

You've guessed it...it's time for some indicators for performance management. All phases within the employee journey are tricky, but I would say this is quite a delicate topic, because even though it's a professional environment it touches on personal aspects (your competencies, your "enough-ness", how good you are and how good you feel you are doing things versus how others see it).

Some indicators you might want to use:

- Average yearly scores of performance management by business area or unit

- Breakdown of overall performance ratings and by business area

- Percentage of line managers that feel well equipped to give feedback

- Percentage of goal completion per person and per business area

- Retention rates within the organization

- Offboarding questions around fair treatment from line managers, respectful feedback, etc (We will cover this during offboarding phase as well)

- Special time for #UXingTheSh*tOutofEXAlert because it's about how a person feels, thinks, does and says (It's always about this, but a bit more in this case!) Look for qualitative answers on how they feel regarding their process (Do they feel valued? Are they recognized enough for their efforts? Does the feedback they get resonate with them? Is the process fair? Are they happy with it?). You can certainly quantify those by using a simple 1 to 5 scale

PHASE V
CAREER PLANNING AND SUCCESSION

There's been a lot of noise around the office lately because gossip o'clock is saying that there might be some organizational changes. HR has neither confirmed nor denied any of those comments through formal comms.

Ramona however, has said there's a "lot of smoke and no barbecue, because people don't read properly." Turns out all it was is that all the managers (herself included) had received a link to fill in a quick survey with five questions and they're already producing all sorts of dramas with it. First question of the survey was a dropdown list to select your area. Second one, another dropdown list to select your role within that area. Third one was a comment box with the following questions: "What does a high potential employee look like? What are their personal and professional traits?" Fourth was a comment box to state the name of their "natural successor" for the role their currently in. Catherine's thought about this before, a no brainer actually. Lastly, there was another comment box asking for suggestions for HR to support the business on career planning and succession (Looks like they're asking other people to do their job for them?! But she has to admit it also feels nice to be asked, they never asked her about this before).

Her answers looked something like this:

1.   Marketing

2. Marketing Senior Manager

3. Someone who is amazing doing their job and getting things done and is not afraid to go the extra mile. However, they're not just about work, this person needs to have a good understanding of their strengths and flaws (so they don't play against them). They have self-control, are team players and care for others. They are not afraid to say they don't know something, but while they say this they're looking for ways to learn. (Did she just describe herself? Hell yes. She's no 3, Adam).

4. Sam Hunt

5. Give the business some guidance on how to deal with career management and succession planning. Sending out a survey like this with no prior explanation is ridiculous and has caused unnecessary noise around the business. Do you have a strategy for this? If so, we'd love to hear it. What are the next steps after the survey? Are you sharing the answers with the whole organization?

(She wrote: GET YOUR SH*T TOGETHER!!!, but deleted it before hitting submit because she is a professional – most of the time!).

She's curious about Adam's answers. Can she find out? Nah, too much hassle. But she can sense that the successor would be Antonio (Because he's "easy to work with", also known as: doesn't say anything when Adam gets his tantrums in front of the team and does what he's told).

In terms of planning Sam and Katrina's careers, she's played it by ear just like she did in her last workplace. There was no clear guidance from HR so she's basically used her previous experiences as line manager and gut feeling to identify what they needed to learn, and how they would do it. The occasional and informal chats about where they see themselves in a couple of years had happened (especially during after office drinks). She's also encouraged (nagged) them to present some of those learnings at team meetings. Adam was not thrilled about "wasting" 15 minutes of his precious meetings, but she didn't care much, she did it anyway and she's proud of the kids (Exhibit A that's she's not easy to work with like Antonio, and also a better line manager!)

Two months have gone by since the survey, HR has not sent anything again around this topic. She asks Adam about it, his answer: "They must be busy planning the year-end party, sweetheart."

CATHERINE'S EXPERIENCE

PAIN POINTS

* **GETTING NO GUIDANCE FROM HR OTHER THAN THE EMAIL AND STRAIGHTFORWARD ONLINE QUESTIONNAIRE**

* **SHE'S STILL DRAGGING HER BAD EXPERIENCE FROM HER PERFORMANCE MANAGEMENT REVIEW** and now she's comparing herself to her peers and annoyed by the assumption that she is not Adam's first choice

DELIGHTS

* **RAMONA'S FRESHNESS TO SAY IT LIKE IT IS,** plus now she's got a new favorite phrase to use ("All smoke and no barbecue")

* **DESPITE FEELING SHE'S DOING HR'S WORK FOR THEM,** she's glad to have been asked for her opinion in who should be the next Catherine at Company A. Sam deserves all the shots in the world when she decides to leave!

* **OFFERING THE KIDS DEVELOPMENT OPPORTUNITIES.** Yay her!

* **ANOTHER CHANCE TO COMPLAIN ABOUT HR** (Let's face it, we love it!)

THINK ABOUT YOUR OWN EXPERIENCE AT THIS PHASE OF THE EMPLOYEE JOURNEY, WHAT WERE YOUR P&Ds?

BUSiNESS PAiN POiNTS - CAREER PLANNiNG AND SUCCESSiON

Some organizations have the luxury to hire a consulting firm to assess their career planning, build their succession strategy and general initiatives. They offer a main "umbrella" plan, and also design ad hoc baby umbrella plans for each area. Each of these deliverables tends to go against invoices, so the organization better get its money's worth!

For all the other organizations, there's the HR department to sort this out and do a "Light career and succession planning" combo (Sometimes annoyingly spelled as "Lite"). This is done at the risk of building generic one-size fits all that end up fitting nobody (There is no such thing as the Sisterhood of The Travelling Pants in real life!).

Lack of specific guidelines create a big opportunity for informality and open interpretation of the few initiatives around this employee journey phase. The survey in Catherine's experience came with no previous warning on the objective, so it managed to ruffle some organizational feathers. And the worst part of it all? There's been no further sharing after it was conducted.
Another common situation is when a line manager leaves and they think: "Let's give the direct report a chance" but alas, the direct report was not ready yet and got burnt. When facing a new professional challenge people need to feel equipped not only on a hard skills level, but also on a soft skills level.

HR PAiN POiNTS - CAREER PLANNiNG AND SUCCESSiON

Remember the quick sample gauge with the HR Ninjas presented at the beginning of the book? This was the phase within the employee journey they thought HR struggles with the most / is the hardest to get right. It is no surprise it was closely followed by performance management, because they're two sides of the same coin. I agree with the HR Ninjas because, for full disclosure purposes, this phase within the employee journey is the one that I have yet to see being implemented 100% successfully by HR. I've seen a lot of good-intentioned sparks and many fancy strategies that were destined to live in the HR repository (I am guilty of this as well).

Now that people tend to leave organizations faster than before (nudged by an aggressive market and a bad employee experiences), it's harder to keep up with the ambitious career planning, let alone succession planning. But then again if they're leaving so fast... HR has a fair degree of responsibility in it. Ouch us.

ADRESSiNG THE PAiN POiNT - CAREER PLANNiNG AND SUCCESSiON

The first thing that needs to be addressed is the housekeeping aspect: do performance management well (with indicators, fairness, and objectivity) and then move along to the next level for career planning and succession. If you haven't identified who your top performers are (so your "golden children on the 2.1% with their upper 5 rating), there's no way you can progress.

Even though it's a no-brainer that a career path in Finance is very different from a career in Tech or HR, there must be common ground for the three paths. The best starting point for this common ground is found in three things: organizational values, desired behaviors and similar role nomenclature standardization. Once this is agreed and signed-off with leadership, HR has the responsibility to lead and move forward into supporting the different areas to build their ad hoc career paths.

More options are available now, because it's no longer an "up or out" approach to planning a career, there can be lateral movements within the same organization that are great development opportunities. This can be quickly identified if there is a formal process established, which ideally would include conducting competency assessments and taking performance reviews into account. But we're oh so busy planning the year-end party...

Career planning and succession management need to be design by an HR department who is joint at the hip with the business areas. Not only because that's the only way to get the leadership's sponsorship, but also to understand what the different roles within the area take care of and how they operate on a high level. It's not only about how well you do your job at this moment (performance management) but also how well you will do it tomorrow (potential). Today's skills will not be enough for tomorrow.

Bruce Anderson knows that all too well and he's done a bit of the legwork for us. He has listed a total of 15 skills that will be required for the future. For hard skills he considers: Blockchain, Cloud Computing, Analytical Reasoning, Artificial Intelligence, UX design (*cough*), Business Analysis, Affiliate Marketing, Sales, Scientific Computing and Video Production. In terms of Soft skills, he suggests that Creativity, Persuasion, Collaboration (*cough*), Adaptability (*cough change management*) and Emotional Intelligence.

Some indicators you might want to consider are:

- Number of promotions per year (breakdown per area)

- Number of people who presented themselves for promotion but didn't progress

- Perception of Fairness on career progression (Also linked to Performance Management fairness)

- Performance ratings (same as above)

- Number of high potential employees identified by line managers and HR

- Gap between desired future skills and current skills

- Line managers' perception of readiness of employees for the next level (Please don't Dracarys anyone at work!)

- Number of critical positions within organization

- Risk of loss of critical positions (High / Medium / Low)

- Likelihood of "flight" from critical positions (High / Medium / Low)

- Time to promotion (How long does it take on average for an employee to get to the next level of the ladder. Useful to breakdown by area)

- Value of the mentor role within career development

- Number of mentoring sessions delivered within the organization

- From our #UXingTheSh*tOutofEXAlert: Talk to people, Rainbow! Get their perception of how fair the promotions are, how aligned is the behavior of someone who has been promoted to the values of the organization. And key as always: get their improvement ideas! We are getting closer and closer to "Ready, Set, Go!". Almost time to get practical with this!

PHASE VI
OFFBOARDING

Catherine has been at Company A for three years and she's starting to feel like she's outgrown the role (plus she just bought an apartment. On her own. Send help). She's also done with the micromanagement and tantrums around the office.

She's doing her LinkedIn research again and is writing down a couple of "doctor's appointments" in her calendar. One of those "appointments" has had a positive answer and they want her to start ASAP. But ASAP actually means in a month, which is shorter than the required 3 month notice period at Company A. Yikes.

Adam receives the news very calmly (against all odds) and says: "I'd be lying if I'd say I'm surprised, just make sure to leave everything in order for Sam and Katrina to pick up." They set the date and send the email to HR to confirm.
Her last month goes as slow as ever. Sam and Katrina are sad she's leaving because overall she's been a better manager than most at Company A (although this was never relevant during her performance feedback sessions). And she's made sure to leave all her documents in an organized way (it's her legacy to the kids!). Although, if possible, she will try to take both of them with her for her new team...

For her exit interview, some random HR Business Partner (let's call her Rando) has found a 30 minute slot to have an "Informal chat" about her experience at Company A over the last three years.

Where the f*ck is Susan? What about no-smile Thomas? Rando hasn't booked a room so they just sit in one of the tables around the office, very public for an exit interview... WTF.

She starts by telling Catherine that all the information will be held in confidence and that she's free to say whatever she wants. But alas, she doesn't leave any space for Catherine to even nod she's understood that, and quickly moves to the questions:

Q1: What was your favourite thing about Company A?
A1: My direct reports and the IT guys

Q2: What was your least favourite thing about Company A?
A2: The lack of innovation and the misunderstanding for the word passion
(She was expecting another question off the back of her answer, but there wasn't any... moving along to Q3)

Q3: Did you have all the tools you needed to do your job?
A3: Almost all
(Again, she's asking for no more details?)

Q4: On the scale of 1 to 5, how good was your manager
A4: A solid 3
(... She's already annoyed at this stage. Why does she even bother if it seems they won't do anything with this information?)

Q5: How would you describe our organizational culture
A5: It's ok, looks shinier from the outside, to be honest

Q6: On the scale from 1 to 5 how helpful has HR been throughout your journey with us?
A6: 3

Q7: Would you say you've been treated fairly in your time with the company, say... during your day to day, performance management reviews, etc. Again, from 1 to 5...

A7: 3

Q8: Would you consider returning to Company A?

A8: Never say never...

Q9: Would you recommend Company A?

A9: Yeah, I guess

The last question they ask her is what would she say to J-Mac if she found him on her way out on the last day. Her answer is "Nothing," although she would probably say that Ramona deserves a raise, that he should review their values and definitely their performance management process. Also, that their leadership team doesn't know how to walk the talk and that HR has proven to her that they try but still miss the mark.

Before she returns her laptop she takes 5 minutes to write her goodbye email. She has a lot to say but will keep it short and sweet. She thinks about the kids while she writes it, so she does it all in a positive tone. She hits send, and goes to turn in her laptop to Wilmer Santos, who is surprised to see her go. "I thought you'd stick around for more than three years, I was rooting for you to take Adam's place!" So was she, but here we are...

Off she goes to her long weekend before starting with Company B (Yes, the ones that ghosted her in the first place!). She certainly wishes Company B will be better than Company A. Her new boss seems nicer than Adam and Ruth combined. And please let HR have more competent people!

CATHERINE'S EXPERIENCE

PAIN POINTS

* **THE WHOLE EXIT INTERVIEW IS A PAIN POINT ITSELF.** Who holds an exit interview in a break-out area?! This is such bad practice it hurts, no wait...she's not hurt, she's angry!

* **CATHERINE CONSIDERS HERSELF A DIRECT PERSON, AND SHE'S ACTUALLY HAD TO KEEP HER REAL THOUGHTS TO HERSELF BECAUSE RANDO DOESN'T SEEM TO GIVE A SH*T.** The fact that she didn't have a familiar face (like Susan or no-smile-Thomas) holding her hand through the exit interview made the experience more stressful and less honest

DELIGHTS

* **ADAM'S WILLINGNESS TO GIVE HER A MONTH TO CLOSE CAMP INSTEAD OF MAKING HER HONOR THE 3 MONTH PERIOD HAS MADE HER VERY HAPPY**

* **WILMER SANTOS MAKING HER FEEL SPECIAL, YET AGAIN!** He should be in HR, he would have booked a meeting room for the exit interview

* **NO DELIGHTS FOR HR :(**

THINK ABOUT YOUR OWN EXPERIENCE AT THIS PHASE OF THE EMPLOYEE JOURNEY, WHAT WERE YOUR P&DS?

BUSINESS PAIN POINTS - OFFBOARDING

One of the biggest pain points for business areas when a person leaves is the loss of knowledge of how things are done. Especially when there is no ad hoc templates within the organization to document this. If the vacancy is not filled soon by HR's recruitment process, it's very likely that the team will be spread thin and stressed out with additional tasks the leaver left (If it's the worst case scenario, they don't even know where to start with them!).

Non-HR areas have little input on what gets asked on exit interviews as they tend to be seen as "standard" everywhere ("Well, why don't they ask us about it?"). And don't get me started on if they ever get the results of their leavers back...

Line managers from non-HR areas might individually know why their direct report is leaving (because of what the report said, or from a personal hunch, or due to gossip!). However, they don't have a breakdown of the reasons they leave (better salary, more challenging job, because of them, etc). Knowing this can make their offers to potential new candidates more robust and also enhance the hiring process.

HR PAiN POiNTS - OFFBOARDiNG

The higher the rate at which employees leave an organization (turnover), the more work there will be for HR for offboarding. So if you haven't done an effective and collaborative job on the previous phases, good luck Rainbow!

Another point of frustration is when you have a hunch (just like the guys from the business) that the leaver is not telling you the truth about why they are leaving. And you question if it would be better to just send out a survey rather than investing 30 minutes of your valuable time in an interview with an employee that is a Rando to you, and you are a Rando to them. This is another situation where you might find yourself singing "Let it go" from Frozen because you can't force people into trusting you (Shocking, isn't it?)

If it's an exit survey, data is not that much work because it's highly likely that it will come through a system already within your beautiful Excel spreadsheet. With interviews, there is additional work to be done (which you can do live and type while you get the answers, previously disclosing that you will be listening and typing at the same time and if that's OK with the leaver!). It does however - as most things in life!, take time and effort to analyze the data and come up with detailed breakdowns for the different business areas.

ADRESSiNG THE PAiN POiNTS - OFFBOARDiNG

In David Sturts' words: "As important as onboarding and building loyalty is, we need to devote similar energy to what we do when employees leave". Your offboarding process has to be as structured, respectful and engaging as possible. It's like you're breaking up with your significant other, and you still care about them. It might be a painful process but I'm sure you'd like to see them go at ease, having said all they needed to say rather than full of regret and anger.

From a selfish perspective, you don't want your ex to drag your name through the mud, do you? If you break up in bad terms with an employee, be sure that he or she will drag your brand through more than mud! Whether the employee has resigned to the organization (Like Catherine) or if the organization has terminated the employee, they deserve to be heard. They deserve to feel that you are listening and that you care about what they have to say. Plus, they might have one or two good ideas on how to be better at this HR thing...

Be respectful, honest and open about the process and what type of questions you will ask and why. It never hurts to say that you understand that they don't know you and you can't expect them to fully trust you from meeting you once, but they can trust that you will do your best to understand their reasons without judging (Only say this if you mean it, if not they'll smell the bullsh*t very fast!)

According to Susan Heathfield, some the most common reasons why employees leave organizations have to do with the relationship with the line manager or the coworkers, unchallenging work, lack of opportunity to use their skills, overall corporate culture and lack of perception that their work does contribute to the organizational goals. It is vital to keep the business updated with why people are leaving, and the way you analyze and present it will (or will not) open the door for HR to become a strategic partner. The data wants to be used and investigated, not to be saved forever as "Leaversinput2020whogivesash*it.xlsx" So get crackin', Rainbow. Analyze the sh*t out of it.

Some indicators you might want to consider for the offboarding process:

- Percentage of completed exit interviews or surveys

- Breakdown of roles leaving the organization (What level are your leavers? From which areas?)

- Leavers' average time within the organization

- Breakdown of the most common reasons why employees leave the organization (even better if you present this specifically for each business area)

- Percentage of leavers who would consider coming back to the organization

- Percentage of leavers who actually come back

- Retention rates and turnover rates

- Number of improvement initiatives delivered off the back of the exit surveys

- Percentage of leavers who do knowledge transfer sessions with their teams

- And also... #UXingTheSh*tOutofEXAlert

THE HEART OF IT ALL <3
ORGANIZATIONAL CULTURE AND CHANGE MANAGEMENT

CULTURE

One of the most genius phrases I've heard about organizational culture has to be the one by Peter Drucker: "Culture eats strategy for breakfast." I love it because he couldn't have been more spot-on! Some people have pushed it to "Culture eats strategy for breakfast, lunch and dinner." And they are also spot-on.

Another thing that I love about that quote is that when you do a quick Google search on it, you will get lots of images of Pac-Man going after the ghosts (Fun fact: the ghosts have names: Inky, Pinky, Clyde and Blinky). If your Culture Pac-Man is hungry and toxic enough, it will definitely eat your Inky Innovation attempts, your Clyde Change initiatives, your Pinky People and even your Blinky Business. That is how strong culture is.

All Pac-Man and llama-ghosts aside (and to bring a bit of seriousness back), The Chartered Institute of Personnel and Development (CIPD) defines culture as the shared characteristics among people within the same organizations and it includes not only values and behaviors, but also routines, traditions, perceptions and beliefs of individuals. It's like every organization is a country, with their currency, their language, their national heroes, their folk stories, political structure, economical systems, and so on.

In his article "Six Components of a Great Corporate Culture", John Coleman advocates for the importance of organizational culture and explains how it can account for a difference of up to 30% in corporate performance when compared with competitors that are culturally unremarkable. He's identified six common components of great organizational cultures: vision, values, practices, people, narrative and place.

Vision is that "simple" phrase that guides the organization towards its goals. It provides a purpose that will be the compass for the decisions the employees make (as long as this purpose is shared and cared for!). Values, on the other hand, are the core of the culture. This is about how you behave and what mindset you have. Practices feed from the values and this is where inconsistency can shine brightly when there's no alignment between vision and values. Seems obvious, but People are the ones that embed the culture and learn it, they stick around longer when they fit the environment. There's a process of reinforcing each other, and it's not by chance that leaders have such an impact on how things are done and how people feel within an organization. I will stress this point further because it is key.

Narrative is the story the people in the organization keep telling themselves about how they are and how they identify, what they like and what they don't Lastly, Place has to do with the architecture, aesthetic design, how things are and how they look.

All these six components are part of the employee journey and you can identify them all within each phase. Think about Catherine's journey as a point of reference. **But most of all, think about your own experience within your organization and answer the following questions:**

- What is the vision?

- What are the values?

- What are the common practices?

- How are the people within the organization?

- What are the common behaviors? What are the most recognized and valued behaviors among employees?

- What is the narrative? What is the story people keep telling themselves about the workplace and how it operates?

- How does the organization communicate with its employees?

- How much trust do the employees have on their leadership team?

- What does the place look like? What stands out?

And the most important question: Are these factors aligned? How so?

The CIPD (Yes, my beloved CIPD again) summarizes pretty well why culture matters. It matters because it offers a way for employees to understand and learn about their organization, to voice (or not) their views, and to connect through purpose (or lack thereof!).

They also mention that according to research, the link between organizational culture and performance is weak. However, a continuous assessment of the culture can help HR gauge how connected people are with the purpose and values, what behaviors are the stars and what story people are telling. This all affects engagement and performance. And we know performance drives good organizational results, so...let's agree to disagree on that one CIPD!

DiD YOU SAY LEADERSHiP?

The easiest way to gauge leadership within organizations is through direct line managers. As usual, I will be (over)sharing my experience on the topic. Since starting my professional life I've had sixteen managers (Sounds like a sh*tload, but I'm counting not only direct managers within the organizations I worked as an HR professional, but also the people I was reporting to within project structures in consulting). I've taken the liberty to categorize them in three basic groups: bad, ok and exceptional.

My estimate looks like this:

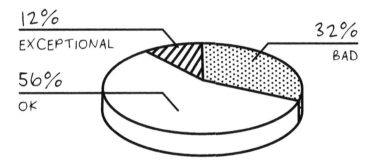

LUCIA'S MANAGERS' DISTRIBUTION

12% EXCEPTIONAL

32% BAD

56% OK

Before I elaborate further on leadership, I want to ask you (once again!) to think about your own experience with your direct managers throughout your professional life. What percentage of them would you say were bad line managers? How about OK? And lastly, were there any exceptional line managers in your life? (Also known as "unicorns").

Please use the graph below to do a rough estimate of your experience:

YOUR MANAGERS' DISTRIBUTION

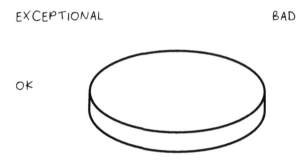

EXCEPTIONAL   BAD

OK

For me, those managers who were exceptional (12%) had four main characteristics in common: they were fair and respectful, they listened and cared for me on a professional and personal level, they shared their knowledge, and they trusted me completely to do my work. If any of them reached out today and asked me to jump, I'd say "How high?"

The ones that were ok (56%), were nice people within and outside of work. But they were lacking three things to be exceptional: complete trust towards my work, knowledge sharing (they weren't that generous) and sometimes even fairness.

The bad ones (32%) shared four main traits: misalignment between the walk and the talk, rollercoaster moods (one day they love you, the other one they hate you), they micromanaged, and they bullied people. Not fun, huh?

It's not a coincidence for me that all the exceptional ones belonged to the same organization, same happened with most of the bad ones. This says a lot about culture and how the values translate into practices, and the power that leadership has to shape everything within an organization.

Find one word to describe your organizational culture. I'll give you a couple of ideas while you think of yours...most common ones I've heard are: toxic, innovative, strong, traditional, people-oriented, aggressive. It's highly likely that you would use the exact same word to describe your leadership team (Is your mind blown or what?).

I would say that Catherine's experience with Company A's culture has been just "OKish". The tardiness and the misalignment between the walk and talk (shared behavior), and her manager's micromanagement and lack of support to drive new ideas made her ghost "Run b*tch, run!" Off to Company B...

Indicator-wise, you could measure on a simple "Strongly disagree" to "Strongly Agree" scale based on the employees' perception on:

- Are all the employees treated fairly?

- Do you identify yourself with the organization's values and behaviours?

- Do you trust the formal communications you get from the organization?

- The leadership team does a good job with communicating to the teams

- How aligned is the walk to the talk (values vs behaviours)?

- How proud are they to work in the organization?

- Is there a team spirit within the organization?

Some other indicators can be more of a "Sharing is caring" situation:

- What three words would they use to describe the organizational culture?

- What are the priorities of the current values according to the employees?

- What are the common traits among the leadership team? (Both good and bad)

- #UXingTheSh*tOutofEXAlert. Talk to people, and get their ideas on how to improve the culture. For example, if we say we are all up for Innovation, but don't allow our employees to execute their new ideas how do we shorten the gap between the walk and the talk? (I'm not saying eliminate it because I'm being realistic, baby steps...)

CHANGE MANAGEMENT

Think about the last five years of your life. I'm pretty sure a LOT has happened during those years. You've probably changed simple things like your hairstyle (for better or worse!), upgraded your wardrobe (for better or worse as well!) or learned new things at work and life. Other changes might have been more complex and harder like changing a job, ending or starting a relationship or losing a person you cared for deeply. In parallel to your personal life, your work life doesn't stop and keeps running, and it might have thrown a couple of additional changes your way that you have to manage and deal with. You might have gone through a new system implementation or updates to your current system's functionalities, a restructure process, a redundancy process, a new team, you name it...

When I talk to clients or colleagues about Change, I like to (over)share a personal story, a story that got me the nickname "The bride" with one of my client's team...you probably know where this is headed. I used to flash out the natural change curve that looks something like this:

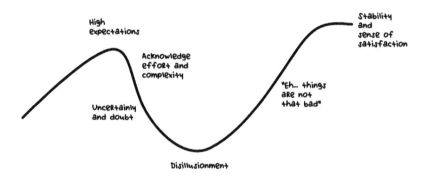

I used to tell the story of my engagement and how my marriage was going (hence, the fitting nickname). It went something this:

Ricardo popped the question while we were on a beach holiday. I didn't even answer his question because I was too busy crying my eyes out (People always ask if I was expecting the proposal, the answer is no, but turns out my parents and my close friends all knew about it). So there we were, engaged. We had high expectations about how the whole marriage thing was going to go, what we would do for the wedding, how we would furnish our apartment, make it a home to both of our liking (He's into anime, I'm into unicorns...you get the picture), decide what to bring, start adulting together by paying taxes and utility bills, etc, etc.

Soon enough we realized it was going to be quite tricky (acknowledging the effort and complexity), not only timewise with both of us working full-time but also budget-wise. As time went by, I had yet another struggle (and this is where I always said that I hope Ricardo never hears this, but now he's probably reading, so I'm sorry Cheerio!). I started questioning if he was the one or if there might be someone else out there and even if I wanted to get married at all.

That was a decision process for me, and probably for anyone who has decided to spend their life with their significant other. I decided to go through with the wedding, and he's been and still is the one (Yes you are Cheerio!). When we finally moved into our apartment together there was a bit of a disillusionment moment. All that partying and honeymooning for this? We were both a mess in our own way and getting on each other's nerves to say the least. We started a bit of a negotiation and established some home rules to ensure we wouldn't kill each other in the upcoming months. And then I would finish saying that after a while, we've found a sense of stability and have seen the light at the end of the tunnel. I couldn't have been more wrong about this.

Today, I still (over)share this story but with a twist, and in a more accurate way (again, the importance of iterations!). The change curve is no longer a curve and it looks like this:

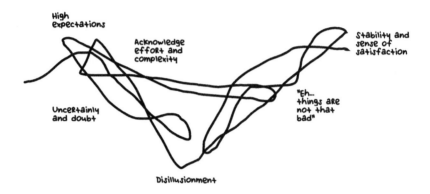

High
expectations

Acknowledge
effort and
complexity

Stability and
sense of
satisfaction

"Eh...
things are
not that
bad"

Uncertainly
and doubt

Disillusionment

As you can see, there isn't one particular and set time for having high expectations, or for recognizing the effort, or getting a sense of stability, or any of the others. We certainly transition through them and that depends on our personal experiences, on how we feel, what we think, do and say (we're such complex creatures!). I tend to have high expectations on a regular basis (Ricardo can vouch for that!), or maybe be in a situation where I never make it to the sense of stability, or I do and then go back to disillusionment. The arrival of our beagle kids (Obbie Wanda and Pancho Taquito) made its very own change path, our move from Lima to London another one, and so on. We're always transitioning through change, for better or worse.

Let's move from my personal life back to the organizational life. Imagine your organization is implementing a new system (SAP, Oracle, D365, Concur, an ad hoc system, whatever it is). How you face it depends a lot on your previous experiences. Some people get great expectations and quickly realize they're not being met, so they get disappointed and won't get out of there until they get proper training and "see the light" at the end of the tunnel. They might think they're all fine now, but maybe something happens that can't be solved by what they learned on their training sessions and they go back to recognizing the effort of having to learn again or reach out for help. Others might not even get high expectations and start right off from a place of uncertainty and doubts because in their previous workplace they implemented a new system and it was basically a sh*t show on wheels. Very few will reflectively say "this too shall pass, let's embrace it!", and go from recognizing the effort straight to finding their sense of stability in the newness. These rare specimens are what I call "Northern Light stakeholders" (you have to be very lucky to get to see them!). To sum it up: We face change based on our previous experiences, we don't respond the same way to change, and we can jump around that "curve" depending on what we think, feel, say and do.

Catherine, our "fictional designated persona" also had her Change Management issues as seen on phase three (L&D). Her team doesn't understand the new system's process for Purchase Orders. They didn't get the right training nor proper communications about the changes and the benefits of the new system. In her words: "A very crappy way of handling changes". What's wrong with this picture?

In 2014 IBM published "Making Change Work While The Work Keeps Changing," a study about change management in organizations. It focuses on what they call The Change Gap, and they worked with more than 1,500 people worldwide in a range of different roles from project managers to change sponsors through surveys and face-to-face interviews. I love this report not only because it's IBM research (and my heart will always have a shade of blue) but because it's still so relevant and I've seen the findings in real life at the projects and organizations I've worked with.

Some of the key findings from IBM's report:

- Only 20% of respondents are considered successful in managing change

- 87% of respondents state that not enough focus is placed on managing change in critical projects

- Only 40% of respondents believe they have the right skills in place to successfully manage change projects in the future

- Most important aspects of successful change are related to soft factors (what we may consider llamas and rainbows): Top management sponsorship, a shared vision, corporate culture that promotes change, honest and timely communication and ownership of change by middle management

- Challenges of implementing change are corporate culture (you know all about that don't you? It's eating your strategy for breakfast and sh*t...), shortage of resources (you probably have experienced this one all too well), complexity underestimation and change of processes / IT systems

While I was working with clients and organizations in their change process, the first priority was to understand their culture (their vision, behaviors, narrative, people, and place). This would allow us to customize the initiatives and try to become native in that environment. A good consultant is a good chameleon and can blend in any setting by recognizing what the client needs, and how they need to get it done. There's no one-size-fits-all.

Stakeholder mapping is a key activity within change management and it normally starts with the leadership team. But good change management maps all the layers, bottom to top. You need to identify:

- Who is whom? Your basic b*tch list of names and roles (A lot of people stop right here and say they've done their stakeholder mapping... ignorance is bliss!)

- How much the change (whatever it is) impacts them and their team? (high, medium, low)

- What is their reaction to the change (Are they fans? Haters? Followers?)

- How much cooperation do you need from them? (100% necessary? Nice to have? You couldn't care less?)

- What are their expectations?

- What are the benefits and potential risks they perceive of the change?

One of the most common mistakes when mapping stakeholders is the lack of frequency by thinking you are ok with a one hit wonder meeting. The second one is not looking after the fans or enthusiasts of the change because you think they're just dandy with the whole thing and miraculously they will stay that way. Big no-no's.

Doing the mapping once at the start of the change journey, once in the middle and once at the end is destined to fail. You need those three interactions (Especially with leadership) but you also need "quick hits", and being around them to identify if their expectations are not met or if their team (or them on a personal level) are changing their mind about how they perceive the change and its benefits or risks. This takes us to the other important part: keeping the enthusiastics happy. It's normal to want to focus and change the hearts and minds of those stakeholders that are roadblocks to the change or that are constantly challenging the progress of change. But don't forget that the happier you are about something or the more you look forward to something, the easier it is for you to feel disappointed if something unexpected happens. Look after your "flock".

All the information you gather from the people impacted by the change helps you build a change case. Which is basically articulating the purpose of the change: the why, the benefits, the effort. And it needs (desperately!) to be linked to the bigger purpose of the organization and be signed off by the leadership team. It's always easy to find the benefits for the organization (efficiency, transparency, traceability, improvements, etc), the real trick is to articulate the benefits on a personal level. Once this is ready to go, it has to be shared and cared for throughout the process of change, as it will be the compass to all the effort and energy that will be put into the change. Make it worth people's while. Build it with them, not for them. If they see their words reflected on the change case, they will certainly be more engaged.

Engagement is a must when facing changes and asking for people's feedback, and ideas usually do the trick. If you're given the chance to bring your ideas to the table, and they're valued and recognized as something the team wants, I'm 100% sure that you would push that baby as much as you could. Firstly, because of a complete sense of pride, and secondly for everyone's benefit!

Communications and training are both key aspects of managing changes (Which were clearly lacking in Catherine's experience). Sending out one piece of communication or uploading some training documents to a shared repository doesn't tick off these two activities at all, despite this being the modus operandi for most Project Managers (Well guess what, Pablo? It's not that straightforward). Morgan Galbraith however, is quite straightforward in his article "Don't Just Tell Employees Organizational Changes Are Coming — Explain Why". He's all about spending time explaining the changes, why they're important and making a compelling case (our Change case as mentioned before). Communication is expected to be not only regular, but consistent and transparent. If there are things you don't know, just say you don't know, but you will try to find out.

I've seen many in leadership positions that are actually scared of admitting they don't know something, despite it being the best way to answer to their teams. The "I don't know" plus the magic words "but, will get back to you on that" and an actual follow-up response are a killer combination to build trust and reinforce consistency. And whether you are HR or not, you should try it!

One of the most significant changes coming our way nowadays is the Digital

Transformation (This whole topic can be a part of #Iteration2...but more likely could turn into its own beast "Digital Llamas"...coming soon on Amazon books- JOKES!). Everyone wants to be "Digital". The real challenge is how they actually make the organization become Digital. And digital is always linked to innovation (which etymologically, means pretty much the same as change, or renewal).

One of my favorite explanations about what being digital means comes from Paul Gibbons. In his book "Impact: 21st Century Change Management, Behavioral Science, Digital Transformation and the Future of Work" (Long ass title, but worth your time!), he starts by stating that "being digital" can mean different things to different organizations, but that it mainly has to do with 5 key ideas: Vision and purpose centered on digital; a digital culture mindset within the organization; using customer experience and employee experience to drive value; building and/or exploiting platform strategies that include connectivity and networks; and taking a comprehensive and systemic approach to opportunities.

Is your organization working towards any of the points above? Chances are that they're definitely trying to. And as you can see, this book is all about employee experience so yay us for being digital! We've got one down.

Another interesting approach to winning the digital disruption comes from Scott Andrew Snyder and Todd Helwin in their book "Goliath's Revenge."

They mention there are six rules to achieve this that I will mention below (and spice up with my comments):

1. Deliver Step-Change Customer Outcomes, a little better than last year is not good enough (This applies for customers and employees if you ask me!)

2. Pursue Big I and Little I Innovation, innovate both top-down and

bottom-up (It's not about getting just the CEO onboard, get Shezaad the Senior Finance analyst onboard as well, after all, he's doing the day to day job, isn't he?)

3. Use Your Data as Currency, you own your data so use it (Data is the most underutilized currency for HR as well, we just saw the pathetic case of Catherine's experience in Phase VI Offboarding!)

4. Accelerate through Innovation Networks, overcome the curse of 'not invented here' (Again, innovation!)

5. Value Talent over Technology, preemptive skill development pays off (My personal favorite, AI, Robotics, and all those fancy things will come for us, but we've got an advantage)

6. Reframe Your Purpose, have the guts to stay focused on what really matters (Change case, change case, change case!)

It's indicator time again! Some indicators you might find useful for change:

- Percentage of people in leadership roles that are supportive of the change

- Percentage of people that understand the change and its impact

- Percentage of people that feel positive about the changes

- How many people within the organization think the organization is good at managing changes?

- Do the employees feel they have been equipped and given enough tools to not only face but embrace the changes?

- How much people understand of the benefits that the changes bring

- How supportive has the line manager been through the change process

- Number of risks versus mitigation activities

- Percentage of success of risk mitigation activities

- Estimate time for employee to be fully "functional" with the new ways of working (i.e. if it's a system or process implementation)

- Tracking activities within the change plan

- #UXingTheSh*tOutofEXAlert. Ask people what can be done differently? What are they happy with? What are they miserable with? What lessons have they learned from change experiences?

READY, SET, GO!

So far we've explored the different stages of the employee journey through Catherine, and how both culture and change management are a big part of how the employee thinks, feels, says and does within an organization.

This last section is all about taking action to get the people at the center of the HR actions through a Design Thinking approach, responding to the employees' needs through initiatives that are do-able, that will be well accepted and that you will be able to measure by getting the yay or nay of your very own internal customers. After all, how can they say nay to something they helped bring to life, am I right?

As a reference, **I will use the five stages of Design Thinking according to the Hasso-Plattner Institute of Design at Stanford (d.school): Empathize, Define, Ideate, Prototype and Test. I will do a brief explanation below as a starting point, and then will expand each section accordingly:**

1. Empathize - This stage is all about your persona, their story and what they're about

2. Define - Set a problem that we could collaboratively solve for the employees. We can state it as a question of how to improve a process, or how to build the best experience we can for a specific situation that HR is in charge of

3. Ideate - This is the moment where everyone gets the chance to do a bit of

'sharing is caring' and bring all the ideas forward (no matter how crazy they might seem, get them rolling). We'll get a chance to discuss how feasible/desirable they are and prioritize accordingly

4.   Prototype - If you bring your best idea to life, what will it look like? What are we doing about it? When do we start?

5.   Test - Show your idea to the world (also known as: your employees!)

This might look easy and like a 1-2-3-4-5 step sequence, but just like with the change curve it's a non-linear process. You might think you're done once you've shown your brand new initiative to your employees but...Think again! We need to gather some feedback and see if there's anything we can do to improve it and make it better (Which might jumpstart a whole new iteration of empathizing and testing!)

For illustrative purposes, I have picked a general problem that everybody in HR should want to solve: How can HR offer the best experiences to our employees? (Quite broad, but we'll refine it as we go!). If you are a non-HR person this is also for you, it can work when you are reviewing a process that you want to improve with your team, your ways of working, etc.

FiRST THiNGS FiRST...

We know the business is always busy and nobody has time to give away, but you will make it work by inviting them way in advance (at least a month!) so they can organize themselves. My suggestion is contacting the leaders of the organization first, letting them know that you want to gather feedback on HR topics (or non-HR topics for that matter! You can be as specific as you'd like), including when you expect the session to happen, who will lead them, why you're doing this, that it will take at least three hours (yes, three at least!), and that you'll share the highlights of the results with them. Offer them a seat at the table if they want to participate, and also ask them to let you know if anyone has any issues with the proposed date. Give them a deadline: four working days to get back to you.

Once you've done this and (fingers crossed) there are no issues, you move along to sending out your communications to the whole organization. Sell it as a collaboration session to make sure HR is listening to the employees and how together you can improve the employee experience (plus, you will make them accountable for it as well). Throw in some breakfast to lure them in, and state that there are limited spaces to join (I'd say no more than 20 people per session, and do at least 2-3 sessions), and that the highlights of these sessions will be shared (And for consistency's sake, you shall share the highlights, this will make you accountable for what you are offering and you will need to deliver to build a good perception on HR's work!).

Get yourself lots of post-it notes, some blue tack, pens, A3 papers and sharpies, reserve a nice, spaceful meeting room and get crackin' with your PowerPoint. Your PowerPoint only needs guiding slides, so make them as attractive as possible and follow your brand's guidelines. Always!

PREPARING FOR THE SESSION

Your session should be built around the following aspects:

1. First and foremost, imagine how you'd like the session to go. Write down what you'd like to get out of it

2. Lure your participants in with the offer of a good breakfast and a good collaborative time. Mornings are always best for these type of sessions

3. Do an Introduction to the session, present the agenda, how long it will take, etc. Be charming AF since the beginning, it's all about engaging them! Acknowledge and joke about the bad reputation HR has, and how you and your team want to fix that for the organization with their help

4. Presentation of the facilitator and brief introductions from the participants

5. The purpose of the session: Why are you doing this? What are you asking for? Link this to the broader purpose of the organization, not just to HR/Non-HR

6. One slide of Design Thinking approach. Could be the five stages + what a persona is + how we will collaboratively to find solutions for our HR pain points. If this is the first time you're facilitating this sort of approach, don't be afraid to say it and ask the audience to "bear with you" and "be kind" through the process

7. Persona: Feel free to use Catherine as an example of how to build this. Make them work in teams to think about their average employee at your organization. This should be very straightforward and they'll certainly have a bit of fun building it. Brace yourself for some funny stuff to come up. Allow playfulness, but also aim for respect! It's a professional environment after all

8. Define: To save some time, you will state the problem, which will be "How can HR offer the best experiences they can to our employees?" To save even more time, you will have selected three of your most "painful" phases of the employee journey, and you will assign it as a question to each of your three groups. Let's use the HR Ninjas' top three answers from which phase of the employee journey they find we struggle with the most / is the hardest for HR to get right as an example:

    a. Team 1 will take "How can HR offer the best Career Management and Succession experience to our employees?"

    b. Team 2 will take "How can HR offer the best Performance Management experience to our employees?"

    c. Team 3 will take top three for now: "How can HR offer the best Onboarding experience to our employees?"

9. Ideate: This is the chance you've been waiting for. Give them the responsibility to come up with engaging ideas on how to solve the question proposed to each team. They need to work this on two levels:

    a. Individual level: Start with the individual approach. Each person has to come up with at least 3 ideas of how to tackle this problem and solve the question

    b. Group level: All the members of the group will share their ideas. Once they've shared them, they need to prioritize them in terms of feasibility and desirability. Once this is done, they need to select their winning idea, which is the one HR could potentially drive forward for the whole organization

10. Prototype: Even though you will do the work of analyzing the results after the session, ask them to draw or write a paragraph or two of how the employee's experience is going to go when their idea is put into place. They also need to present it to the other teams, so caveat that while they're getting their idea ready! Let's say the team's winning idea was a "speed-dating" initiative for performance management, where the employee will get quick feedback from their teams (peers, line manager, line manager's manager, direct reports, etc). Make them draw the sequence of events and what their persona would feel (delight especially) going through that experience

11. Say your goodbyes, your thank you's and your "could we all have a lovely group photo please?"

After the session is done, pat yourself in the back for being brave enough to stand up to do this exercise because it can be scary to hear people propose ideas for your work (Regardless of your potential Mr. Hammonds' in the room). When you are done with this, email that lovely group photo to your participants, and cc' their direct line managers, show off their hard work. If you want to take it to the next level of advertisement: Send an email to the whole organization with the picture and a massive thank you. Plus, a "Watch this space for further updates" to create expectation and commitment (from your side!) to get some actions rolling.

Make sure you are thorough with the input you got from the participants. It's always easy to tabulate the results live in Excel (Rainbow, Excel can be your very very best friend!)

Even if most of the ideas were not chosen as the "winning" ones, keep them anyway as they might spark up a conversation or two later on. Build a plan to deploy one winning idea at a time and share them with the leadership in detail and an overview for the whole organization. Make sure to put the credit where it belongs, Rainbow. Celebrate the results and give updates on any potential improvements, people like knowing that things are happening and that they are getting somewhere, especially if it's for their own benefit as employees!

REMEMBER...

Whether you are an HR or Non-HR person, go back to basics and put people at the heart of the things you do, it's the only way to get good results. Listen to people and invest time in finding ways to engage them in making things better. While you are at it, throw in some llamas, indicators, rainbows, design thinking, tough love, a healthy organizational culture, proper change management, and of course, amazing year-end parties. Easy breazy!

LUCIA ABUGATTAS B.

Born and raised in Peru just like Paddington Bear, but with a Bachelor in general Psychology and a Licentiate degree in Organizational Psychology. Associate Member of the Chartered Institute of Personnel and Development (CIPD) in the UK, with a Level 5 Diploma in Leadership and Management and full-time crazy dog lady permit.

Started her career in Human Resources, specializing in onboarding, employee engagement, leadership development, and internal communications. Later on discovered the joys of consulting with organizations like T-Consult, IBM and KPMG for change management, design thinking, leadership and talent development. Currently living in London with Cheerio (a.k.a. husband), but soon to head back across the Atlantic to reclaim custody of Obbie and Pancho (the beagle kids!)

Printed in Great Britain
by Amazon

26599211R00058